Psalm 119

A Commentary on the Entire Psalm

Cor Bruins

Scripture Truth Publications

PSALM 119

First Published serially in Truth & Testimony magazine 1993-1998

FIRST EDITION

FIRST PRINTING March 2010

ISBN: 978-0-901860-88-0 (paperback)

© Copyright 2010 Cor Bruins/Scripture Truth

Cover photograph © Scripture Truth

Published by Scripture Truth Publications
31-33 Glover Street,
Crewe, Cheshire CW1 3LD

Scripture Truth is an imprint of Central Bible Hammond Trust, a charitable trust

Typesetting by John Rice
Printed by Lightning Source

Editor's Note

I am greatly indebted to Ian Mears and the late Edwin Cross, together with their associates at Chapter Two, who undertook the initial editing of the manuscript.

As the author explains in his Introduction, the Psalm is an acrostic in twenty-two sections, each of eight verses, corresponding to the letters of the Hebrew alphabet in order. Within each section the first word of each verse begins with the same letter. To inform the reader, the English translation of this first Hebrew word is displayed in **bold type** within the text.

Why the Psalm, with its great subject of the Word of God, should be written in this way is a matter of some interest. Was it simply to aid memorisation of the original Hebrew text? Do the individual letters of the Hebrew alphabet suggest themes concerning God's Word which are taken up in the eight-verse sections? Does the current use of the letters of the Hebrew alphabet to represent numbers in dates aid our appreciation of the Psalm? It obviously expresses the hopes and fears of a faithful Jew, but what is in it for those under the new covenant? As you read, in the light of the author's comments, you will no doubt reach your own conclusions. The author's emphasis is on the practical lessons to be drawn from this Psalm. We pray that every reader will come to share his delight in the daily reading of the Word of God and the blessings this brings.

John Rice
March 2010

PSALM 119

4

Contents

PSALM 119

Introduction

This is the longest of all the 150 Psalms, and perhaps for that reason the 176 verses are seldom or never read completely either in public or in private meditation or study. This is a great loss. Although the name of the author and the date of this unique Psalm are not given, God is breathing throughout every precious verse, which unfortunately to many only seem repetitious. The Psalm shows us the various virtues and aspects of the Word of God, which can meet our every need and situation.

SOME INITIAL REMARKS

In some translations there are printed at the head of each section of eight verses a Hebrew letter of the alphabet – א *aleph* (verses 1-8); ב *beth* (verses 9-16); ג *gimel* (verses 17-24); ד *daleth* (verses 25-32), etc. Each of the eight verses of a section begins with the letter that is set at its head. For instance, verses 1-8 all begin with the letter *aleph*, verses 9-16 all with the letter *beth*, verses 17-24 all with the letter *gimel*, and verses 25-32 all with the letter *daleth*.

Furthermore, the meaning of the letter at the head of each section [1] often plays a role in being the dominant theme of that section. For instance, verses 1-8 with the letter *aleph* at their head, which signifies an ox in the service of man, gives us a type of the perfect servant, Christ; verses 9-16 with at their head the letter *beth*, which means a house with foundations, suggest that which is fundamental for the Christian's life; verses 17-24 with at their head the letter *gimel*, which means a camel, suggest a wilderness scene through which the camel passes with enough resources, so they portray believers as they pass through this world's wilderness scene having adequate resources in

---

[1] In general the meaning of the Hebrew letters follows Gesenius [5].

the Word of God. Finally, verses 25-32 with the letter *daleth* at their head, which means a door, suggest the theme 'The entrance of Your words gives light', etc. The composition of this Psalm is therefore in the form of a perfect and regular alphabetic acrostic of 22 sections corresponding to the 22 letters of the Hebrew alphabet, each of eight verses.

It may well be asked, 'Why 22 sections of eight verses precisely?' Here I quote from W Graham Scroggie [12]:

> The word eight, in the Hebrew, is *shmoneh*, from *shaman* which means "to make fat", to "superabound". Seven is enough, but eight is "more than enough", 7 plus 1; it goes beyond seven, and is the beginning of a new series, era, or order. Eight is the first "cubic" number, and is more than a square, which is represented by four. It is the number of resurrection. Christ rose from the dead on "the first day of the week", which was the eighth day, Saturday being the seventh of the Jewish week. The "superabundance beyond completion" is shown in Psalm 119 in respect of the Law of the Lord, the Word of God, in twenty-two stanzas of each eight verses; each verse a couplet, so that, as to lines, each stanza is eight multiplied by two. Nothing could more perfectly display the fertility, fatness, and fullness of the word and will of God.

There are eight other acrostic Psalms:

a. Psalms 9 and 10, but in these the acrostic is defective, some of the letters of the alphabet being omitted. The alphabet runs through the two Psalms; Psalm 9 has the first half of the alphabet, and Psalm 10 gives the remainder with the omission of some letters;

b. Psalm 25 has it also, but is irregular in form;

c. Psalm 34 is defective in one letter only (verse 22);

d. Psalm 37 is a complete acrostic;

e. Psalm 111 and Psalm 112 are complete acrostics;

f. Psalm 145 has one letter missing.

For those interested, let me add that there are two examples of acrostics outside the Psalms. In the book of Proverbs, chapter 31, the twenty-two verses (10-31), describing the virtuous woman, begin with the letters of the Hebrew alphabet in order.

Lastly, in the book of Lamentations the arrangement is similar to that of Psalm 119: the 22 verses in each of chapters 1, 2 and 4 begin with the letters of the Hebrew alphabet in order; and in chapter 3 each group of three verses begins with the same letter. Perhaps the acrostic device was devised to help the memory. No doubt the reader will find it so.

INTERESTING FEATURES

As a diamond has different facets reflecting the light striking upon it in different colours, so bringing out its beauty, this Psalm also shows different facets of the Word of the Law of God. There are a number of these facets to be distinguished:

1. verse 1. *torah* – 'law' from the root meaning to teach, or instruct. This word occurs 25 times and is always in the singular (never 'laws'). See verses 1, 18, 29, 34, 44, 51, 53, 55, 61, 70, 72, 77, 85, 92, 97, 109, 113, 126, 136, 142, 150, 153, 163, 165, 174. It has the meaning of teaching, guiding, directing, instructing. It is a divine instructing with regard to conduct and character.

2. verse 14. *eduth* – 'testimony'. It is a revelation or a revealed psalm. It occurs 9 times in verses 14, 31, 36, 88, 99, 111, 129, 144, 157 (all in the plural except 88). The word *edah*, also translated as testimony, occurs 14 times in verses 2, 22, 24, 46, 59, 79, 95, 119, 125, 138, 146, 152, 167, 168 (all in the plural). It means a testimony, or a reiteration, an attestation or witness – a constant witness to Jehovah's nature and will: what God is and what we ought to be.

3. verse 4. *pikkudim* – 'precepts' or 'commandments'. It occurs 21 times in verses 4, 15, 27, 40, 45, 56, 63, 69, 78, 87, 93, 94, 100, 104, 110, 128, 134, 141, 159, 168, 173 (always in the plural). It means a charge given to us by God for which we are responsible. It is connected with words meaning to place in trust, or to take oversight.

4. verse 5. *khukkah* or *khok* – 'statute'. Sometimes a 'portion' (as for the priests in Genesis 47:22; also 'task' as in Exodus 5:14). The word occurs 22 times in verses 5, 8, 12, 16, 23, 26, 33, 48, 54, 64, 68, 71, 80, 83, 112, 117, 118, 124, 135, 145, 155, 171. It comes from the root meaning to cut into, to hack, hence to engrave, to carve, see Job 13:27 'You set a limit (literally, inscribe a print) for the soles of my feet.' 'You have marked out to my feet how far they shall go.' It has the idea of that which is established, or definite, an appointed portion of food, or task. It is a definite limit, as in Job 26:10 and Proverbs 8:29, an appointed law, statute or ordinance. It is therefore a divine direction to obtain my obedience, or to arrest disobedience. It stimulates obedience. It is the Law as the permanent record of God's will.

5. verse 6. *mitzvah* – 'commandment'. It occurs 22 times – see verses 6, 10, 19, 21, 32, 35, 47, 48, 60, 66, 73, 86, 96, 98, 115, 127, 131, 143, 151, 166, 172, 176. It comes from the root to command, and has the idea of prohibition also. It is a divine imperative decree. Examples of this are found in the fact that God forbids Adam eating from the tree and that God tells Noah to build the ark. It is a command imposed by God's absolute authority. It shows us the requirement of His will.

6. verse 7. *mishpat* – 'judgment'. The word occurs 22 times in the following verses: 7, 13, 20, 30, 39, 43, 52, 62, 75, 84, 91, 102, 106, 108, 120, 121, 137, 149, 156, 160, 164, 175. It means the sentence of a judge in verse 75 and 137. It is especially used of a sentence by which a penalty is inflicted, and it is therefore a judicial sentence, a decision the Lord makes.

7. verse 9. *dabar* – 'word'. It occurs 24 times in verses 9, 16, 17, 25, 28, 42 (twice), 43, 49, 57, 65, 74, 81, 89, 101, 105, 107, 114, 130, 139, 147, 160, 161, 169. It is similar in meaning to the Greek word *logos*. It means therefore the 'articulation of God's will to men'. It is the spoken word (like the 'oracles of God' in 1 Peter 4:10-11). The Ten Commandments are literally the 'Ten Words' or Decalogue (Exodus 34:28). It is therefore a medium for communicating the revealed will of God.

8. verse 11. *imrah* – a 'saying' (Arabic *amr* – a thing). It can also mean a poetic word, or speech. It is a word, a speech, or also a sacred hymn, or poem, as in Psalm 17:6. It occurs 19 times in verses 11, 38, 41, 50, 58, 67, 76, 82, 103, 116, 123, 133, 140,

148, 154, 158, 162, 170, 172. Finally, it is something communicated orally, the words by which a revelation is imparted.

9. verse 1. *derekh* – 'way'. It has the meaning of walking, a going, hence a journey which any one takes, a way, a path in which one goes (Arabic *tariq*, or *sabil*), a mode or course. It occurs 13 times in verses 1, 3, 5, 14, 26, 27, 29, 30, 32, 33, 37, 59, 168. Finally, it can mean a road as trodden, a mode of life, a course of action marked out by God's Law.

It is interesting that in only three verses is there no direct reference found to the Law or any of its synonyms; theses verses are: 90, 122, and 132. Another interesting fact is that the name Jehovah occurs 22 times, though not necessarily in each of the 22 sections. (Some expositors count 24 times).

The Psalmist refers to himself 325 times. We might almost say that this Psalm is too individualistic to be regarded as written simply to represent the nation of Israel but to this I shall refer later. One expositor has counted 70 prayer requests in this Psalm and encourages the reader to list them. Every verse in section five (verses 33-40) is a prayer.

WHAT OTHERS SAY ABOUT PSALM 119

1. 'All who want themes for soul or service can find them here; for it may be said that every verse embodies a seed thought' (W Graham Scroggie).

2. It is a divine alphabet of love (Johannes Paulus Palanterius [11]).

3. It is a paradise of all doctrine [11].

4. It is the school of the truth [11].

5. It is the ABC of the Christian's Praise (German Bible).

6. 'It seems not to need an expositor, but only a reader and listener' (St Augustin).

7. 'The Psalm rehearses the various virtues of the word of God, and the saints' delight and profit therein. Any believer may generally use it as the breathing of his own soul; but in its full prophetic character, it would seem that it will be the language of the true Israel on their return to God and His long neglected oracles' (J G Bellett [1]).

8. 'Psalm 119 is the expression of the effect of the law written in the heart of Israel, when they had long erred from God's ways and were sorrowing under the effects of it. ... We see thus that the form of this Psalm cannot apply to the Christian. ... But from the general principle we may learn much, as that which is wrought in the heart as regards its moral disposition' (J N Darby [4]).

9. 'Purity of "heart" is not so much in question as purity of "walk". That is, there is everywhere present the evidence of a faith which, when the grace of God is known in truth, purifies the heart of the believer; but the soul has not yet had revealed to it an object to which it can look in peaceful forgetfulness of itself. The darkness still continues, and the true light is wished for rather than enjoyed. It is very manifestly the expression of one who discerned in his inner man the excellent perfection of the law, and whose whole heart, therefore, was set on its attempted fulfilment. The zeal of Jehovah, as that which marks distinctively the spiritual man, is plainly visible through every expression of human

weakness and stress with which the Psalm abounds' (A Pridham).

10. 'That this great Psalm has its many blessed thoughts and exhortations for the individual believer is indeed very true. The 176 verses are all precious gems and many find an echo in the heart and life of a true believer' (A C Gaebelein).

PROPHETIC ANTICIPATION

The Law could not produce in men the obedience that is required by it. Only the cross, if looked at and believed in, shows the complete condemnation of sin, and hence deliverance from it. Now, by the new birth and the indwelling of the Holy Spirit, the very principle of obedience is implanted in us. In Psalm 118 Israel acknowledges the mercy of Jehovah and Him as their Messiah. The moment is to come when the Law will be written on their hearts according to the promise of the New Covenant (Jeremiah 31:31-34). But this is therefore still in the future. Here in Psalm 119 we have an eightfold alphabet. The number eight signifies what is 'new' in contrast to what is 'old'. We have therefore throughout this Psalm too a continual allusion to the 'new covenant'. Every letter of man's language is now taken up to express the praise of that which was but an intolerable yoke and burden before.

PERSONAL APPLICATION

'For what the law could not do in that it was weak through the flesh, God did by sending His own Son in the likeness of sinful flesh (flesh of sin, N.Tr.), on account of sin: He condemned sin in the flesh, that the righteous requirement of the law might be *fulfilled* in us who do not walk according to the flesh but according to the Spirit'

(Romans 8:3-4). It is with this sure knowledge that real Christians, those who have been born again and have the Holy Spirit dwelling in them, can now taste and enjoy the 'blessings' of the new covenant. The Book of the Psalms is not about the Church but mainly expresses the thoughts and feelings of a persecuted Jewish remnant. The position, hopes and future of the church are not found in the Psalms though there is very much in them that is for our instruction and comfort.

I have studied this Psalm with the aim of gleaning from it such help as it may yield for the Christian. I would heartily encourage the readers to study it with me and to get the blessing that comes from doing so. I am leaving aside comments that refer to Israel but hope to point out the essential difference between the author of Psalm 119 and the way he sees things, and the viewpoint of the Christian.

Analysis of Psalm 119

Division One: Verses 1-24
Plentiful resources for the pilgrim journey

1. *Aleph*   verses 1-8   God's Word brings happiness in the way.
2. *Beth*   verses 9-16   God's Word gives power for a holy life.
3. *Gimel*   verses 17-24   God's Word provides resources for trials along the way.

Division Two: Verses 25-48
Strength for the weary

4. *Daleth* verses 25-32   God's Word revives and restores.
5. *He*   verses 33-40   God's Word meets our weakness.
6. *Vav*   verses 41-48   God's Word leads to victory.

Division Three: Verses 49- 72
Our immense spiritual riches

7. *Zain*   verses 49-56   God's Word reveals our spiritual assets.
8. *Cheth*   verses 57-64   God's Word transforms into His image.
9. *Teth*   verses 65-72   God's Word strengthens in adversity.

Division Four: Verses 73-96
Spiritual maturity through daily meditation

10. *Yod*   verses 73-80   God's Word shows us our responsibility.
11. *Kaph*   verses 81-88   God's Word for our security.
12. *Lamed* verses 89-96   God's Word helps us mature spiritually.

DIVISION FIVE: VERSES 97-120
THE IMPORTANCE OF DAILY BIBLE STUDY

13. *Mem*   verses 97-104   God's Word is living water.
14. *Nun*   verses 105-112   God's Word gives direction.
15. *Samech* verses 113-120   God's Word for our support.

DIVISION SIX: VERSES 121-144
IN THE SCHOOL OF THE SPIRIT OF GOD

16. *Ayin*   verses 121-128   God's Word is a well of refreshment.
17. *Peh*   verses 129-136   God's Word gives power for testimony.
18. *Tsaddi* verses 137-144   God's Word brings us near to Him.

DIVISION SEVEN: VERSES 145-168
THE NEED FOR SPIRITUAL RENEWAL

19. *Qoph*   verses 145-152   God's Word is the basis for prayer.
20. *Resh*   verses 153-160   God's Word teaches us Jesus Christ is Lord.
21. *Shin*   verses 161-168   God's Word for power and peace in persecution.

DIVISION EIGHT: VERSES 169-176
CONTINUOUS REVIVAL

22. *Tau*   verses 169-176   Appendix: God's Word for continuous revival.

PSALM 119

Division One

Verses 1-24
Plentiful Resources for the Pilgrim Journey

1. *Aleph*   verses 1-8

    God's Word brings happiness in the way.

2. *Beth*   verses 9-16

    God's Word gives power for a holy life.

3. *Gimel*   verses 17-24

    God's Word provides resources for trials along the way.

א

1. ALEPH - verses 1-8

Meaning: Ox
The first letter of the Hebrew alphabet is *aleph*, which means ox or cow.

Derivation: The name of this letter is derived from its shape in the most ancient alphabet, which represents the rude outlines of the head of an ox. It is still found in the remains of the Phoenician inscriptions, and is taken from the ancient sign of the constellation Taurus, the bull.

Numerical value: One (1)
As a numeral it stands for one, but when there are two dots above it the value is one thousand.

Significance: In the letter *aleph* we have the thought of an ox tamed and accustomed to man and in service to man. God delights in reconciling man to Himself, blessing man, so that he may be accustomed to God, and to other men, living in peace with all men, as Romans 12:18 exhorts. This living in peace with one another is what Jehovah wanted for the 'thousands of Israel' (Numbers 10:36). Lastly, the word for lion is *ari* in Hebrew, also starting with the letter *aleph*.

The first and second letters of the Greek alphabet are *alpha* and *beta*, from which we get our word alphabet. These two Greek letters have no meaning. In the Hebrew language the two first letters are *aleph* and *beth*, and together they form the word *ab*, which means father. This shows how prominent the fatherhood of God is in the Scriptures.

Summary

Right at the beginning of this Psalm we have the type of the Lord Jesus Christ as the one who said, ('I am among you as the One who serves' (Luke 22:27).) And the one who said, 'The Son of Man did not come to be served, but to serve' (Matthew 20:28). He gave Himself, the supreme sacrifice. For the heart of the believer, who sees in Him the burnt offering, He is typified as the ox. This offering typified the greatest appreciation of His Person.

God's Word brings happiness in the way

REASON FOR HAPPINESS: PERFECTION AND PROGRESS

verse 1:   **Blessed** *are the undefiled in the way,*
                Who walk in the law of the LORD!

'O the happiness of those perfect in the way' (YLT). The word for blessed in the Hebrew is in the plural, and describes the state of the undefiled (or perfect). It reminds us of the abundant blessings that are the portion of all true believers in Christ: ('Blessed be the God and Father of our

Lord Jesus Christ, who has blessed us with every spiritual blessing in the heavenly places in Christ' (Ephesians 1:3).

A. CONSIDER THEIR CHARACTER: 'PERFECT' (OR, UNDEFILED)

They were not always perfect, but sinners once, every one going his own way, dead in trespasses and sins. But Christ gave Himself as a sacrifice for sin, to redeem sinners both from the guilt and power of sin. It is interesting that the ox signifies the greatest measure of appreciation of the Person and sacrifice of Christ in the book of Leviticus. This Psalm begins by reminding us of the blessed Person of Christ and His worthiness and greatness and what He means to the Father. Here in this first verse the Lord Jesus Christ is brought before us as the supreme sacrifice for sin. The last letter of the Hebrew alphabet is the letter *tau*, which means a sign or a cross. We see therefore that the Psalm begins and ends by reminding us of the Person and death of Christ on the cross for sinners, that they might be perfect before God in Him. The word perfect has the meaning of blameless, complete, whole, entire, sound (Exodus 12:5; Leviticus 3:6; Psalm 19:7).

B. NOTICE WHERE THEY WALK: 'IN THE WAY ... IN THE LAW OF THE LORD'

In Isaiah 53:6 we read, 'we have turned, every one, to his own way'. That was in their unconverted days. Now they are the Lord's. They have found the true way: 'Jesus said, "I am the way, the truth, and the life"' (John 14:6).

C. SEE HOW THEY ARE MAKING PROGRESS

After being born again there must be growth. Not only have they found the way, but they are walking in it. They are making progress. (The Hebrew verb for walking is *halakh* and has the meaning of going on, going forward.) 'Blessed is the man who walks not in the counsel of the ungodly' (Psalm 1:1). This is very practical. We are in

Christ and 'As you have therefore received Christ Jesus the Lord, so walk in Him, rooted and built up in Him' (Colossians 2:6-7).

REASON FOR HAPPINESS: A DOUBLE BLESSING

verse 2: **Blessed** *are those who keep His testimonies,*
Who seek Him with the whole heart!

A. THEY 'KEEP HIS TESTIMONIES'

Remember what we said about this word 'testimonies'? It testifies of what God is, and it also shows me what I ought to be. Before we can *keep* His testimonies, we must first have received them, accepted them and be willing to obey.

B. THEY 'SEEK HIM WITH THE WHOLE HEART'

Notice that they seek Him, they seek to please Him, to be more like Him. This is not merely an intellectual activity, but it is a question of the whole heart being engaged. My heart yearning after Him day by day, all day long. 'And you will seek Me and find Me, when you search for Me with all your heart' is the wonderful promise (Jeremiah 29:13).

REASON FOR HAPPINESS: A DOUBLE PURPOSE

verse 3: **They also** *do no iniquity;*
They walk in His ways.

A. NEGATIVE: 'THEY DO NO INIQUITY'

As they keep His testimonies, and seek the Lord with their whole heart, staying close to Him, they do not sin. It is not characteristic of a true Christian that he practises sin (1 John 3:9). Rather, an act of sin in the life of a believer is considered an aberration, totally uncharacteristic of his position. 'If anyone sins, we have an Advocate with the Father, Jesus Christ the righteous' (1 John 2:1).

B. POSITIVE: 'THEY WALK IN HIS WAYS'

They walk with Him, and in His strength. He is the way in which they walk – like Him. 'He who says he abides in Him ought himself also to walk just as He walked' (1 John 2:6). The effect of abiding in Him is seen in our walk.

THE SECRET OF HAPPINESS: COMPLETE SUBMISSION

verse 4:   **You** *have commanded us*
            To keep Your precepts diligently.

There is first of all *complete submission*. Remember that a commandment is a divine imperative decree, it's an order. Whether to Adam or to Noah, they had to submit. Adam did not, but Noah did submit. Are we willing to submit our will to His will? This submission is not imposed upon us, we are not forced to submit to our Lord Jesus! That would be servile. No, it is because we love Him that we willingly and gladly submit to Him. The verse continues: 'to keep Your precepts *diligently*'. There is nothing superficial about this submission! It is not a partial submission, but complete. There is no reserve, no holding back part, no hesitation, but a glad and wholehearted surrender.

THE SECRET OF HAPPINESS: COMPLETE ABANDON

verse 5:   **Oh, that** *my ways were directed*
            To keep Your statutes!

Then there is a *complete abandon*. This is a prayer! It is the deep longing of the heart expressed in a sigh! There is a profound consciousness of complete weakness and inability of ourselves to do anything that is pleasing and acceptable to God. Here is a cry for assistance, for help, for power! Surely the Lord hears such a sigh! Surely the Holy Spirit will direct you and me to 'keep Your statutes', to do His will and not our own! A statute is a divine direction to obtain our obedience, or to arrest disobedience.

THE SECRET OF HAPPINESS: COMPLETE CONFIDENCE

verse 6:   **Then** *I would not be ashamed,*
When I look into all Your commandments.

Lastly there is *complete confidence.* 'Then' – consequently! He has learned from experience! He has learned from past mistakes. He has learned that he will not be ashamed, when he has 'looked into' ('respect unto', AV) all the Lord's commandments! He says as it were: 'Yes, looking back I am ashamed of those times when I acted in self-confidence and in my own strength and wisdom, and failed miserably. But now I have learned not to have this self-confidence, but to have complete confidence in the Lord.' We must learn not to pick and choose with regards to the Lord's will for us. All His ways are blessedness and peace, all His will is good and acceptable and perfectly suited to our needs.

THE HAPPY RESULT: LEARNING TO PRAISE

verses 7:   **I will praise** *You with uprightness of heart,*
When I learn Your righteous judgments.

We saw in verse six that he had learned some very important and useful lessons. Here in verse seven we see what more he has learned by submitting himself and surrendering himself to the Lord. He has learned the Lord's 'righteous judgments'. What does that mean? His righteous judgments are the decisions He makes concerning right or wrong, which give expression and put into execution the righteous character of God. We have much to learn about His judgments. We must learn that He always judges righteously, never arbitrarily or with any prejudice as men judge. We must learn from Him now on earth how to judge like Him, so that later, when we shall reign with Him a thousand years, we shall be able to put into practice what we have learned. Whatever He thinks best is good and right, even when He must discipline as a tender and compassionate Father. One day, when we shall stand before His judgment-seat to be rewarded, we shall praise Him with uprightness of heart for all His righteous judgments.

THE HAPPY RESULT: OBEDIENCE

verse 8:   **I will keep** *Your statutes;*
Oh, do not forsake me utterly!

Meanwhile, we continue our walk as Christians here on earth. What should be our ambition? 'I will keep Your statutes', is what the Psalmist says he will do. 'Keeping' means to observe and put into practice. His statutes are His directives to obtain our obedience. 'If you love Me, keep My commandments', the Lord Jesus said (John 14:15). As well as many other things, that means that we love one another with the same divine love that He Himself has poured into our hearts by the Holy Spirit – see Romans 5:5. So there is the divine provision to enable us to do His bidding. All this will keep us humble, realising that of ourselves we can do nothing, as the Lord Jesus said, 'Without Me you can do nothing' (John 15:5). The Psalmist finishes this first section of eight verses with a prayer, 'Oh, do not forsake me utterly', but there is no need for us, New Testament believers, to think that the Lord would ever abandon us or that the Holy Spirit would leave us or be taken from us, for He abides with us for ever (John 14:16). However this should not make us careless, but would encourage us to continue on our way with this constant prayer, 'Lord Jesus keep me close to Yourself.'

ב

2. BETH – verses 9-16

Meaning: House

Derivation: *Beth* means house, which we see in the names Bethel, house of God, and Bethlehem, house of bread. It comes from the root *banah*, to build. This letter has a strong foundation line with a small protrusion at the right hand side, called the 'tittle'.

Numerical value: Two (2)

Hebrew usage: '*b*' alone, put in front of any Hebrew word, means with, or in (and thus has the meaning of abiding, constancy).

Significance: The Old Testament begins in Genesis 1:1 with the letter *beth* and the first word is *bereshit*, 'in the beginning'. *Beth* is the first letter of the word *ben,* which means son, a prominent Old Testament word. The idea this letter gives us is that of solid foundation, the rock on which our houses (our lives) are built (Matthew 7:24). In this section of eight verses we have important foundation truths.

35

God's Word gives power for a holy life

What is the remedy for doubts? Knowing the truth(s) contained in the Bible. Reading and studying the Bible, and so filling our thoughts with the word of God will deliver us from doubts. 'Whatever things are true, whatever things are noble, whatever things are just, whatever things are pure, whatever things are lovely, whatever things are of good report, if there is any virtue and if there is anything praiseworthy—meditate on these things. The things which you learned and received and heard and saw in me, these do, and the God of peace will be with you' (Philippians 4:8-9).

THE WORD OF GOD PURIFIES

verse 9: **How** *can a young man cleanse his way?*
By taking heed according to Your word.

Verse 9 begins in Hebrew with *bameh*, which signifies 'with what?'. Here is a soul with a question! The believer has sought to walk pleasing to the Lord, but he is conscious of the world around him with all its defiling influences. There has been defilement in thought and imagination. Some believers suffer from unclean thoughts or unclean suggestions from the enemy. This young man has been defiled in this way. Now he asks the question, 'With what shall I cleanse my way, my heart, my thought-life?' This verse gives us the first wonderful fact about the Word: it purifies. 'Therefore, having these promises, beloved, let us cleanse ourselves from all filthiness of the flesh and spirit, perfecting holiness in the fear of God' (2 Corinthians 7:1). 'You are already clean because of the word which I have spoken to you' (John 15:3). 'Christ … gave Himself … that He might sanctify and cleanse her (the Church) with the washing of water by the word'

(Ephesians 5:25-26). The Bible gives us light, and power, and support. We are responsible to keep ourselves from becoming defiled.

THE WORD OF GOD KEEPS

verse 10:   **With my whole** *heart I have sought You;*
Oh, let me not wander from Your command-
ments!

This verse shows us that the Word keeps the believer from wandering. When God's Word is obeyed daily it will keep me from being deceived, and it will purify me from the defilement of having to walk through this world full of uncleanness. 'With my whole heart I have sought You.' We have to be in earnest about it! To rush in and rush out of the Lord's presence for a little reading and prayer is not what we might call properly a 'Quiet Time'. We must take time to be holy. Notice that the second half of this verse is a prayer, 'Oh, let me not wander.' We have a prayer in verses 5, 8 and this verse. Prayer and Bible study go hand in hand.

THE WORD OF GOD IN MY HEART

verse 11:   *Your word I have hidden* **in my heart,**
That I might not sin against You!

Someone has said of this verse that we have here:

a.   the best thing – Your Word;
b.   in the best place – my heart;
c.   for the best purpose – that I might not sin against You.

What a precious jewel of a verse! What a good thing it is therefore to memorise scripture, so that we may be able to quench all the fiery darts of the enemy with the sword of the word and say, 'It is written.'

THE WORD OF GOD IN MY THOUGHTS

verse 12: **Blessed** *are You, O LORD!*
Teach me Your statutes!

This does not mean that mere man can bless God in the sense of imparting something to Him Who is all-sufficient. But the sense of the word blessed in the Old as well as in the New Testament is that He is worthy 'to be praised, to celebrate with praises'. Thus we acknowledge His goodness, with desire for His glory. The Lord Jesus was that blessed Man on earth Who said, 'If you abide in My word, you are My disciples indeed. And you shall know the truth, and the truth shall make you free' (John 8:31-32). There are various ways in which we may learn the truth:

1. by faithfully reading and studying it day by day;

2. by the ministry of the Word through God-given teachers;

3. by reading commentaries written by gifted and spiritual men.

Through these means of grace the Holy Spirit can teach us the will of God, for He is that teacher. Let us therefore echo the prayer of the Psalmist, 'Teach me Your statutes', and remember that the meaning of a statute is 'a divine direction to obtain our obedience, and to keep us from disobedience'.

THE WORD OF GOD UPON MY LIPS

verse 13: **With my lips** *I have declared*
All the judgments of Your mouth.

'With my lips I have declared', begins the verse. The believer may speak in 'living echoes' of His words. He must first be able to speak to us, before we can speak to others what He has told us. We do well to remember this. Before Jesus can send us forth 'to preach', He calls us first to be 'with Him' (Mark 3:14). Perhaps it is good to ask ourselves, 'What do I use my lips for?' Certainly not for tale-bearing? How we need to pray daily, 'Keep watch over the door of my lips' (Psalm 141:3; see also Job 27:4).

THE WORD OF GOD IS MY JOY

verse 14: *I have rejoiced **in the way** of Your testimonies,*
As much as in all riches.

'I have rejoiced in the *way* of Your testimonies.' When we remember that the meaning of testimony is that which testifies of Him, speaks of Him, what He is and what we ought to be, the focus is therefore on Him. We rejoice in Him and the way in which He leads and guides us. Is it true that we really delight to please Him and to live for Him? Is reading the Bible a real pleasure for us, or simply a daily duty? How do we profit most from our daily Bible readings? Here are some suggestions that may help. Before we read, we ask for the Lord's help and illumination. When we have finished reading we may ask the following questions:

1.   Is there an example in my reading I must follow?

2.   Is there a commandment I must obey?

3.   Is there any sin mentioned that I must avoid?

4.   Is there a promise that I can claim by faith?

5.   Is there a new thought concerning the Lord Jesus Christ?

Of course we can make up our own list, but the important thing is that we meditate on what we have read, chew it over and take it in.

THE WORD OF GOD FOR MY CONTEMPLATION

verse 15:   *I will meditate **on Your precepts**,*
               And contemplate Your ways.

Here is a determination expressed, 'I will meditate.' How important it is to be determined about maintaining a daily Bible study. Many Christians are so disorganised that they cannot find time for Bible-study, or rather, that's their excuse. We can always find time for something that we really want to do! The important thing is that we do find some time each day. The Psalmist says, 'My voice You shall hear in the morning, O LORD; in the morning I will direct it to You, and I will look up' (Psalm 5:3). '... *and contemplate* (or *have respect unto,* AV) *Your ways*'. It is apparently not enough to be interested and meditate on the Word, but it should be followed by putting it into practice. To 'have respect' is to be willing to obey the word of God.

THE WORD OF GOD MEMORISED

verse 16:   *I will delight myself **in Your statutes**;*
               I will not forget Your word.

How important it is also that we do no forget what we have read: 'I will not forget Your word.' In verse 11 we saw the need for hiding it in our hearts. To store the mind with the word of God is the true way of victory. Of the Lord Jesus it was said that the Word was in His heart. How can the Holy Spirit possibly bring anything, any word, from the Bible to our remembrance if we have not first stored it there. Nowadays we say that the computer will give you nothing but what you have first stored in its memory! Some Christians take verses of scripture out of their context. Take for instance Luke 12:12, 'For the Holy Spirit will teach you in that very hour what you ought to say.' These believers take this verse to mean that you do not have to prepare yourself in order to minister the Word of God. They do not think that any preparation is necessary. I am convinced that the true spiritual believer does his daily Bible study and so the Holy Spirit prepares him, whilst the believer stores his mind with the Word of God. Then, when a believer is called upon to minister that Word, the Holy Spirit will bring to his remembrance what he should say.

And by the way, the verse in Luke 12:12 had to do with and was fulfilled in the apostles when they were persecuted as we find it recorded in the book of Acts. So everything really depends upon our appetite for the Word of God. Our verse says, 'I will delight myself'. The writer of this Psalm certainly gives us a good example to follow. He repeats the fact that he delights in the Word of God at least 8 times: see verses 24, 35, 47, 70, 77, 92, 143, 174. In 1 John 2, the apostle John says to the young men, 'you have overcome the wicked one', and 'you are strong, and the word of God abides in you, and you have overcome the wicked one' (verses 13-14).

Notice the 'actions' in verses 15 and 16 of our Psalm:

a.   I will meditate;

b.   I will contemplate (have respect);

c.   I will delight;

d.   I will not forget.

ג

3. GIMEL – verses 17-24

Meaning: Camel

Derivation: In Phoenician monuments, on the coins of the Maccabees, and in the Ethiopian alphabet, this letter's shape bears a resemblance to the neck of a camel.

Numerical value: Three (3)

Significance: The root idea of this letter/word is 'to give, do, or show good or evil to any one'. (The associated word for camel is probably derived from its common use as a means of carrying goods.) In a positive sense it means 'to deal bountifully' or 'to load with benefits'. We find this meaning in the name Gamaliel, which means 'the reward of El (God)'. It shows us the wealth of God's revelation given to us in His Word, the precious Bible. All the spiritual supplies and refreshment we need for our wilderness journey are found in that precious living Word.

God's Word provides resources for trials along the way

PRAYER FOR ABUNDANT LIFE

verse 17: **Deal bountifully** *with Your servant,*
That I may live and keep Your word.

The Christian pilgrim has started his wilderness journey (verses 1-8), and has asked many questions (verses 9-16). He has understood that as he continues in the way of the Lord he will undoubtedly meet with difficulties and problems that must be dealt with. He realises therefore his deep need of help from the Lord and His divine guidance for his path. The Lord Jesus has said that He Himself is the 'way' for us (John 14:6), and in John 10:10 He says, 'I have come that they may have life, and that they may have it more abundantly.' The Psalmist can only pray that Jehovah will deal bountifully with him, so that he might live. We as Christians can thank our Father for having blessed us with every spiritual blessing in the heavenlies in Christ. We have all that God could give in Christ. What wonderful resources! What abundant life! In verses 9-16 we see a young man, still rather inexperienced, and with overwhelming needs. In verses 17-24 he realises he is a 'stranger' (verse 19) and needs to be shown the way. No wonder that he prays, 'give me fulness of Your strength and life so that I may do Your will and keep Your word.' James tells us, 'If any of you lacks wisdom, let him ask of God, who gives to all liberally and without reproach, and it will be given to him' (James 1:5). In order to be able to keep His word, we must know the enablement of the Holy Spirit.

PRAYER FOR ILLUMINATION

verse 18: **Open** *my eyes, that I may see*
Wondrous things from Your law.

Here is an earnest pleading with the Lord to give insight and spiritual illumination: 'Open my eyes.' In Mark 8:22-26 we read about a blind man near Bethsaida whom Jesus healed and the way the healing proceeds is very interesting and instructive. After the Lord's first action, He asks him whether he can see, and the man answers, 'I see men like trees, walking.' Obviously he had sight now, and he could see. But his seeing was far from what it should be. So a further act of Christ was necessary. The man was given the power of sight, then the power to use his sight in order to distinguish one object from another. This suggests the progressive manner in which the truths of scripture are perceived. '... *that I may see wondrous things from Your law.*' The Gospel opens the eyes to the knowledge of spiritual things, but then there is a further enlightening necessary of the 'eyes of your heart' (Ephesians 1:18, N.Tr.) to apprehend the spiritual blessings we have in Christ. Are we discovering wondrous truths in the Scriptures day by day? Never approach the reading or study of the Bible without this prayer: 'Open my eyes.'

PRAYER FOR KNOWLEDGE

verse 19: *I am* **a stranger** *in the earth;*
Do not hide Your commandments from me.

One of the precious truths we shall discover when studying the Bible is the fact that we are 'strangers in the earth'. Some questions will be asked as we study:

1. Who am I?
2. Where do I come from?

3.   What is the purpose for my being here on earth?

4.   Where am I going?

5.   Am I ready for my eternal destiny?

Once, when still in our sins, we were '… aliens from the commonwealth of Israel and strangers from the covenants of promise, having no hope and without God in the world. But now in Christ Jesus, you (we) who once were far off have been brought near by the blood of Christ' (Ephesians 2:12-13). Now here is a prayer that the New Testament believer never needs to pray – 'Do not hide Your commandments from me' – because there are no longer any mysteries hidden as far as New Testament believers are concerned! The apostle Paul writes, 'How that by revelation He made known to me the mystery (… by which, when you read, you may understand my knowledge in the mystery of Christ), which in other ages was not made known to the sons of men, as it has now been revealed by the Spirit to His holy apostles and prophets: … to make all see what is the fellowship of the mystery, … that now the manifold wisdom of God might be made known by the church to the principalities and powers in the heavenly places' (Ephesians 3:3-10). The Spirit of God delights to make known to every believer what was in the heart of God from before the foundation of the world. We see that in verse 18 there is the prayer for open eyes and in verse 19 there is the desire for an open Bible, i.e. to be illuminated by the Holy Spirit. This is how the Christian progresses in the way through this world.

PRAYER FOR SATISFACTION

*verse 20:   My soul **breaks** with longing
For Your judgments at all times.*

The word *garas* means 'to crush or to break in pieces' and so we have this strong expression, 'my soul breaks with longing'. It is a deep desire for the word of God and the will of God. Paul expresses such a desire for Christ: 'That I may know Him and the power of His resurrection, and the fellowship of His sufferings, being conformed to His death' (Philippians 3:10). 'As the deer pants for the water brooks, so pants my soul for You, O God' (Psalm 42:1). This is not just an emotional moment, it is a constant longing 'at all times'. It is sometimes said, 'You are what you long for.' What is it that we must long for? 'Mary, who also sat at Jesus' feet and heard His word ... has chosen that good part, which will not be taken away from her' (Luke 10:39, 42).

A REBUKE TO THE PROUD

verse 21: **You rebuke** *the proud—the cursed,*
Who stray from Your commandments.

There are some elements which are directly opposed to that which is spiritual. These are elements that would rather deceive and lead astray. Pride, self-sufficiency and independence of God are arch-enemies of spiritual progress and understanding. The Lord Jesus gives this direction, 'Take My yoke upon you and learn from Me, for I am gentle and lowly in heart, and you will find rest for your souls' (Matthew 11:29). Of all moral sins, the Lord Jesus considered pride one of the worst and most hateful. There may be the pride of race, or the pride of face, or the pride of place, but the worst is the pride of grace – to have a superior attitude towards other Christians and pretend to be more spiritual than they are, perhaps because of more light and understanding of the Scriptures. There is a danger in much knowledge, even in much Bible-knowledge. The apostle Paul warns against this, 'We know that we all have knowledge. Knowledge puffs up, but love edifies' (1 Corinthians 8:1). Actually, proud persons are very miserable because no one loves them since they keep themselves so aloof. Never forget that *pride* was at the root of Satan's fall: '… lest being puffed up with pride he fall into the same condemnation as the devil' (1 Timothy 3:6).

A REPROACH FOR THE GODLY

verse 22: **Remove** *from me reproach and contempt,*
For I have kept Your testimonies.

The apostle Paul says in 2 Timothy 3:12, 'Yes, and all who desire to live godly in Christ Jesus will suffer persecution.' Today it is not easy for the believer to be faithful in this sin-sick world. To believe in God, that Jesus Christ is the eternal Son of God, that the Bible is true and that Jesus is the only way of salvation, brings much scorn and reproach. There must therefore first of all be:

1. A definite choice and decision of heart: 'all who desire to live godly' (a life that pleases God);
2. No surprise that we 'will suffer persecution'; and
3. The knowledge that all our resources to remain faithful are 'in Christ Jesus'.

If we are treated with contempt, let us not meet the flesh with the flesh and retaliate. Let us rather turn to the Lord and lay our case at His feet and then be positively occupied with His will and Word and leave our defence with Him. It may not be that He will remove the trying circumstance, but He will surely give grace to bear it.

IGNOBLE NOBLES

verse 23: *Princes* **also** *sit and speak against me,*
But Your servant meditates on Your statutes.

Look at the contrast in this verse. There are the princes and there is the servant. Which of the two is more noble? Both are occupied – the princes in speaking evil, and the servant in meditating upon God's statutes. The princes of this world have sat in judgment on the Son of God: '… the wisdom of God (Jesus Christ, see 1 Corinthians 1:24) … which none of the rulers of this age knew; for had they known, they would not have crucified the Lord of glory' (1 Corinthians 2:7-8). If the unbelieving world has treated our Lord Jesus Christ like this, will they treat His followers any differently? Are we willing to be known as His disciples? Think of the attitude of the disciples in the Acts: 'Now, Lord, look on their threats, and grant to Your servants that with all boldness they may speak Your word' (Acts 4:29). This is no prayer for deliverance from their enemies, but a prayer that the Lord might give them even more zeal to continue their positive Christian service in witness for Him.

HUMBLE COUNSELLORS

*verse 24:   Your testimonies **also** are my delight
And my counsellors.*

The positive attitude is continued in this verse with this conjunction of determination – also! The believer is undaunted and fearless, because he is strengthened and encouraged by the Lord. But let us remember what we read in 1 John 2:13 about the young men who were able to overcome the wicked one. It was because they abode in the Word and the Word abode in them that they were strong and able to stand and resist. This section ends with this positive thought: 'Your testimonies also are my delight and my counsellors.' Verse 16 also mentioned this same attitude. He will keep me, as I keep myself in the love of God!

Division Two

VERSES 25–48
STRENGTH FOR THE WEARY

4. *Daleth* verses 25-32

        God's Word revives and restores.

5. *He* verses 33-40

        God's Word meets our weakness.

6. *Vav* verses 41-48

        God's Word leads to victory.

ד

4. DALETH – verses 25-32

Meaning: Door

Derivation: This word means 'door' in the Hebrew, which appears to have been the most ancient form of this letter.

Numerical value: Four (4); which speaks of universality.

Significance: The spiritual significance of this letter seems to be that of entrance, giving entrance, or opening up the way – something which includes and excludes. The way we are in seems blocked, we are at a dead-end, emotionally we may be at our wit's end, deeply depressed and discouraged. *Daleth* will help us discover the way to being revived, restored and encouraged.

God's Word revives and restores

EARTHBOUND!

*verse 25:   My soul **clings** to the dust;*
Revive me according to Your word.

'*My soul clings to the dust.*' What a discovery to make! Indeed, how much value do we attach to the things of this earth? Do we theorise about the Christian life, and yet live for this earth, rather than for the Lord Jesus? What are our priorities? Do we cling to some kind of idol that we cannot let go of? We have tried so hard to get free from this thing, this particular weakness or temptation, but to no avail. We are depressed about it. Romans 7:18 is right when it says, '... for to will is present with me, but how to perform what is good I do not find.' Well might we echo the cry, 'Revive me.' That reviving is in the Life of Christ, lived out in us. Have we surrendered to Him, have we come to Him?

CONFESSION FIRST!

*verse 26:   I have declared **my ways**, and You answered me; Teach me Your statutes.*

Have we told Him all? Our failures, our vain efforts? Our struggles and defeats? Have we left anything unconfessed? Are we willing to judge the root-cause of our defeat? Confession is not only that I tell the Lord my faults, but that I accept myself as I really am, without any pretence and without any excuses. This is a necessary lesson we must learn. 'Teach me ...' continues our verse. Teach me the plague of my own heart (1 Kings 8:38). He 'is able to keep you from stumbling, and to present you faultless before the presence of His glory with exceeding joy' (Jude 24).

WE MUST BE TAUGHT AND UNDERSTAND BEFORE WE CAN TALK TO OTHERS

*verse 27:   Make me understand **the way** of Your precepts; So shall I meditate on Your wondrous works.*

In verse 26 the Psalmist asks to be taught because he is conscious of his ignorance. He lacks experience of many things. Now he asks, 'Make me understand.' To be taught is not enough, we must also grasp and understand what

51

we have been taught, otherwise our knowledge is simply theoretical. We can have an intellectual grasp of the Bible, have knowledge, but lack the wisdom (that comes from experience) to be able to impart that knowledge to others. In order to be able to 'talk of His wondrous works' (AV), we must have inwardly digested the truths of God's word. Too many assume they are teachers because they possess a certain amount of Bible knowledge. But there is something lacking in their talk, their teaching. Before what I say to others can grip them, it must have gripped me first. Paul says to Timothy, 'But you must continue in the things which you have learned and been *assured* of, knowing from whom you have learned them' (2 Timothy 3:14).

BEWARE OF SELF-OCCUPATION

verse 28:   *My soul **melts** from heaviness;*
                Strengthen me according to Your word.

There is nothing more disheartening and discouraging than to be occupied with oneself. Our spirits will begin to wilt and droop. Something has happened to us, and we just wonder, 'Why me?' We cannot understand why the Lord has allowed this. We begin to sulk. We become depressed and burdened with heaviness. In Romans chapter seven the personal pronouns I, me, myself are repeated 47 times. I ask you, with whom is the man in that chapter occupied? The capital letter 'I' is repeated 28 times! There is your answer. He is occupied with self. Let us then follow the Psalmist in his prayer: *'Strengthen me according to Your word.'* Occupation with Christ, with the word of Christ, will get us out of our depressions!

BEWARE OF HYPOCRISY

verse 29:   *Remove from me **the way** of lying,*
       And grant me Your law graciously.

Of course, I can refuse the truth about myself! But that is a form of dishonesty before the Lord, as well as before others. Have you never felt like a hypocrite when you have talked about your spiritual experience with others and that same day you had been unfaithful to the Lord? We can hide our own spiritual destitution from others, but why try to hide it from Him? The Psalmist appeals to the law. But we know that the law can only condemn me and make me see even more my own wretchedness. But no, it is grace we need: *'and grant me Your law graciously.'* It may seem strange to find these two here joined together – law-grace! The literal Hebrew rendering is, 'and favour me with Your law.' If Jehovah favoured His people by giving them a written revelation of Himself in the law of the Ten Commandments, then how much more have we been favoured in Christ by being shown God's wonderful grace of forgiveness of all our transgressions and grace to do His will! If the law shows me what I am by nature apart from grace, then grace shows me what I have become in Christ – 'accepted'. So then, it is no longer I, but Christ. Let us be occupied with Him then!

DETERMINATION

verse 30:   *I have chosen **the way** of truth;*
       Your judgments I have laid before me.

It is up to us now! There must be a choice! God does not do for us what we can do for ourselves! We can stay in our depression and keep on sulking and murmuring and get more and more depressed. But we need not. *'I have chosen the way of truth'* is his decision! Spiritual advance and growth is not automatic! It demands our co-operation, an action of our will. 'Do you want to be made well?', said the Lord (John 5:6). The prodigal son said, 'I will arise and go to my father' (Luke 15:18). Here is the conviction that God's word shall govern our lives – 'Your judgments I have laid before me.' We have that same expression of determination in Psalm 16:8, 'I have set the LORD always before me; Because He is at my right hand I shall not be moved.' Have you made that decision yet?

DEVOTION

verse 31: **I cling** *to Your testimonies;*
O LORD, do not put me to shame!

What a wonderful contrast with verse 25! There he was clinging to the dust. Here in verse 31 the same verb is used, *davak*, but now he is seen clinging to the word; that which testifies of what God is and what he should be. Here is true devotion – clinging to the Lord. That is what Barnabas exhorted the believers at Antioch to do, 'he ... exhorted them all, that with purpose of heart they would cleave unto the Lord' (Acts 11:23, AV). The determination of verse 30 is continued here. '*O LORD, do not put me to shame*', need never be the prayer of the New Testament believer. But we are assured that 'whoever believes on Him *will not be put to shame*' (Romans 9:33).

DEPENDENCE

verse 32: *I will run* **the course** *of Your commandments,*
For You shall enlarge my heart.

The Authorized Version ('I will run the way of thy commandments, when thou shalt enlarge my heart') here makes us think that the Psalmist is striking a bargain with the Lord: '*I will ... when You ...*'; but the above is a better rendering. Here we have the Lord's enabling. It is because everything depends upon His strengthening us! How dependent indeed we are upon Him for our daily walk. What a wonderful change in his soul has been wrought since verse 25, where we saw him clinging to the dust, so terribly earthbound. But now he is soaring! He is able to run, because his heart has been enlarged, given increased capacity. 'But those who wait on the LORD shall renew their strength; they shall mount up with wings like eagles, they shall run and not be weary, they shall walk and not faint' (Isaiah 40:31). May our prayer be, 'Draw me away! We will run after You' (Song of Solomon 1:4).

ה

5. HE – verses 33-40

Meaning: Window or Lattice

Derivation: The meaning of this letter is not certain but many scholars think it means 'window' or 'lattice' – through which objects are beheld. The word *hē* means 'behold' in the Hebrew, possibly from the form of the letter.

Numerical value: Five (5)

Hebrew usage: When attached to other words *hē* can be a preposition meaning 'the' (not used in Hebrew as frequently as in English), or, as a prefix, to ask a question. In Arabic the letter *he* is used in asking a question: 'Hal?'.

Significance: As a windows or lattice, the letter conveys the idea of letting in the light. The number five suggests man's weakness, because a man with only one hand, that is with only five fingers, cannot do much. A further thought is of grace meeting this weakness. The letter *he* occurs twice in JHWH (Jehovah) and this helps us to understand that God in

56

His grace is meeting, and has met, man's utter inability and helplessness.

God's Word meets our weakness

Here then is a desperate need! Only God can meet our need! But we must go to Him and trust Him implicitly, and let Him do the work that we cannot do. 'For when we were still without strength, in due time Christ died for the ungodly' (Romans 5:6).

MY NEED: TO BE TEACHABLE

verse 33: **Teach me**, *O Lord, the way of Your statutes, And I shall keep it to the end.*

Man is totally ignorant of his true and desperate condition as a sinner. That is why the Holy Spirit must convict us of sin, and open our eyes so that we may see our need! The first thing required of a sinner is his total capitulation, his recognition that he is lost and helpless. The Holy Spirit insists upon the surrender of our self-will. The capacity to will and to make decisions remains, but must from now on be under the control of the Holy Spirit. Notice the five-fold prayer from a man who is conscious of his helplessness (remember that the letter *he* is the fifth letter of the alphabet):

1. verse 33: 'Teach … and I shall keep it'
2. verse 34: 'Give me understanding, and I shall keep Your law'
3. verse 35: 'Make me walk … I delight …'
4. verse 36: 'Incline my heart'
5. verse 38: 'Establish Your word to Your servant'.

All these verses express his desire to be taught and to receive light and illumination from the Lord. Let us therefore not be wise in our own eyes, or think we know better than the Lord, but repeat with the Psalmist, 'Teach me, O LORD, the way of Your statutes.'

MY NEED: A CONTRITE SPIRIT

verse 34: **Give me understanding**, *and I shall keep Your law;*
Indeed, I shall observe it with my whole heart.

The desire to be teachable goes together with a contrite spirit! We should take a humble position before the Lord. Our intellect is certainly not to be set aside. The Holy Spirit's activity is to renew our understanding and our mind (Romans 12:2). Even though our intellect must be engaged, yet we must realise that the heart must be involved first of all. In spiritual matters the Bible tells us that we think not with our brains (intellect), but with our heart as the centre of our total being. This is figurative language of course. So when our human, sanctified spirit is taught, our whole heart becomes engaged in the observing. Putting teaching we have received into practice is a question of the heart and the will. And notice it is the whole heart that is engaged in this: 'Indeed, I shall observe it with my whole heart.' This emphasises concentration. The Holy Spirit is our divine Teacher: 'But you have an anointing from the Holy One, and you know all things.' 'And we know that the Son of God has come and has given us an understanding, that we may know Him who is true; and we are in Him who is true, in His Son Jesus Christ' (1 John 2:20; 5:20).

MY NEED: CONCENTRATION

verse 35: **Make me walk** *in the path of Your command-ments,*
For I delight in it.

The need for concentration has been noticed in the previous verse. Here this thought is continued, 'Make me walk in the path'. It is my duty to keep yielding myself to the teaching of the Spirit, and present my members as instruments of righteousness to Him. We are no robots programmed to go through certain motions automatically. 'For it is God who works in you both to will and to do for His good pleasure' (Philippians 2:13). There is always God's side first but also there is most definitely man's side and responsibility. If *He* is going to 'make me walk', I must make it my delight to do His bidding!

MY NEED: A YIELDED HEART

verses 36: **Incline** *my heart to Your testimonies,*
And not to covetousness.

Are we really sincere and determined about following the Lord, doing His will and obeying His *Word?* By nature we are all rebels, only thinking of ourselves and doing our own will. That is the reason why he prays, 'not to covetousness.' Now that we are born of God and have His Spirit dwelling within, we need to be re-schooled, i.e. to be taught His will. Now we can see the need for this prayer, 'Incline my heart.'

MY NEED: A SINGLE EYE

verse 37: **Turn away** *my eyes from looking at worthless things,*
And revive me in Your way.

'The heart is often led astray by the eye', is no understatement! If in verse 36 we have a positive request ('incline my heart'), in this verse we have a negative request, 'Turn away my eyes.' How quickly we are defiled by a look! How quickly we are distracted by what our eyes observe, how quickly deviated from the Lord's way for us. So he prays, 'Revive me in Your way.' Here again, the Lord will not do for us what we must do for ourselves. The apostle Paul tells us, 'Make no provision for the flesh, to fulfil its lusts'

(Romans 13:14). Someone has said that it is the second look that is sin [6]! He meant that, when you walk in the street and you see an unclean thing, a pornographic picture, you cannot help that. But when you stop, or turn to look again, that is deliberate! By turning, or stopping to look again we are actually making provision for the flesh.

MY NEED: STABILITY

verse 38: **Establish** *Your word to Your servant,*
Who is devoted to fearing You.

There must be a fixity of purpose in our hearts. 'For he who doubts is like a wave of the sea driven and tossed by the wind' (James 1:6). 'That we should no longer be children, tossed to and fro and carried about with every wind of doctrine, by the trickery of men, in the cunning craftiness of deceitful plotting' (Ephesians 4:14). The more we are 'rooted and grounded' in the Word of God, the less vulnerable we shall be to deception. There is no excuse for ignorance of the Word. The Lord Jesus clearly said that we must 'watch and pray' lest we be deceived. It is therefore the responsibility of every believer to read and study the Word, so that he might be well-grounded and well-established in the Word of God. '... *Your servant, who is devoted to fearing You*' is the motivation for seeking to be established in the Word of God. We do not want to grieve the Lord, nor the Holy Spirit. And the fear of the Lord also means that if we disobey then we should certainly fear the discipline that must inevitably follow, because we are children of our Father.

MY NEED: TO FEAR THE LORD ONLY

verse 39: **Turn away** *my reproach which I dread,*
For Your judgments are good.

If we fear His Word, that is, respect it and obey it, we need not fear anyone or anything else. *He* will be with us. No doubt, those who do not fear God and deny even His existence, will ridicule us and mock us and reproach us! It is not easy nor pleasant for the believer to realise that, if he wants to be faithful, he may not be popular. There is definite reproach attached to being a disciple of Jesus Christ. This may be a healthy fear! May be he asks here that he might not suffer reproach for adhering to the Word of God. But reproaches for righteousness' sake are to be rejoiced in. The literal rendering from the Hebrew is, 'Turn away my shame which I fear.' The Psalmist may have thought of the possibility that he might commit some evil act, some unfaithfulness, that would bring shame upon the name of the Lord as well as to himself, and so he beseeches the Lord to keep him from this. A similar thought is expressed by the apostle Paul in Philippians 1:20, 'According to my earnest expectation and hope that in nothing I shall be ashamed, but with all boldness, as always, so now also Christ will be magnified in my body.' What Paul feared was that because of the pressures put upon him by the enemies of the Lord, he might in some measure deny the Lord's claims, and dishonour the Lord. This is indeed a prayer we would do well to pray daily!

MY NEED: TO REALISE MY NOTHINGNESS

verse 40:   **Behold**, *I long for Your precepts;*
              Revive me in Your righteousness.

This whole section of eight verses has brought before us our own nothingness and helplessness. This should not be a temporary and emotional feeling, but our constant realisation! In this verse we have the sense of need expressed again, 'Revive me in Your righteousness.' This is a confession of conscious weakness, and of the need for being revived and strengthened with might by His Spirit in our inner man.

To have said, 'I long for Your promises', would be quite human, but he says, 'I long for Your precepts.' We remember from the Introduction that 'precept' means a charge given to us by God for which we are responsible. We must always remember that privileges are inseparable from responsibilities. The Lord has committed a charge to us, like Timothy, to whom Paul says, 'Hold fast the pattern of sound words which you have heard from me, in faith and love which are in Christ Jesus. That good thing which was committed to you, keep by the Holy Spirit who dwells in us' (2 Timothy 1:13-14). It is the Holy Spirit who helps us in our weakness and helplessness, to strengthen us in order that we might walk in obedience to the Word of God.

ו

6. VAV – verses 41-48

Meaning: A Hook or a Nail

Derivation: The shape of this letter in Hebrew is like that of a nail.

Numerical value: Six (6)

The numerical value of *vav* is six, which in the Bible is the number of man, and it stresses man's limitation in contrast with God's infiniteness. We get the idea of what is individual.

Hebrew usage: This letter is what is called a coordinating conjunction. The English equivalent would be the word 'and' which always joins a series of ideas. The letter therefore connects things together. In the Old Testament this letter *vav* occurs more than 15,000 times!

Significance: The use of a nail is to join things together. The word *vav*, meaning nail, hook or peg, is only used in the book of Exodus, and there in connection with the hanging of the curtains in the Tabernacle. The hooks on which the veil (Exodus 26:32) and door (Exodus 26:37) were hung were made of gold;

and those for the hangings around the court (Exodus 27:10) of silver: reminding us of the deity of the Lord Jesus Christ and His work of redemption. These are indeed the hooks on which all His glory is displayed.

God's Word leads to victory

PRAYER FOR FULL SALVATION

verse 41:   Let Your mercies **come** *also to me, O LORD—*
Your salvation according to Your word.

In the previous section we saw the writer's helplessness and nothingness and his desire for reviving. This section stresses the fact that Jesus, having identified Himself with helpless and needy man, is man's only salvation. This is what the Psalmist realises: his constant need for mercies and salvation. For the Christian it is the same: we have been saved and we are being saved. We have experienced God's grace and mercy, and we continue to need His mercies every day. The Psalmist in these verses fears lest in any degree the Lord would withhold His favour from him. This is a needless fear for the true Christian. We may become unfaithful, but He abides faithful, He cannot deny Himself. In salvation we have become identified with the Lord Jesus Christ, and as long as we realise our constant need of Him, and abide in Him, we shall experience victory over Satan and sin and self 'according to Your word'. In 1 John 2:14 we see that the young men were able to overcome the wicked one by the fact that they were made strong through the Word that abode in them.

PRAYER FOR VICTORY OVER SATAN

verse 42:   *So shall I have **an answer** for him who*
reproaches me,
For I trust in Your word.

Here we are told who is the one the Psalmist wants to
answer – 'him who reproaches me'. The verb 'reproach' in
the Hebrew has the sense of 'scorn', 'to carp'. We all know
that Satan is described in the Bible as 'the accuser of our
brethren' (Revelation 12:10). Satan also uses human
beings to inflict scorn on their fellow-men. Unbelievers
may scorn and mock the believer, or ask him tricky questions. The verse continues to tell us that only because the
Psalmist 'trusts in Your Word', will he be able 'to have an
answer'. Here then is another secret of victory over the
enemy, 'But sanctify Christ as Lord in your hearts, and
always be ready to give a defence to everyone who asks
you a reason for the hope that is in you, with meekness
and fear' (1 Peter 3:15).

PRAYER FOR TRUTH THAT OVERCOMES

verse 43:   *And take **not** the word of truth utterly out of my*
mouth,
For I have hoped in Your ordinances.

His desire has been to be able to give his testimony even
before those who oppose him and scorn and ridicule him.
He dreads the possibility that for some reason he would
not have a word to answer – 'the word of truth utterly out
of my mouth'. Only daily experience of fellowship with
the Lord and study of His Word will prepare us to be His
witnesses. Sin in the life takes away our testimony.
Sometimes, even when out of fellowship with the Lord,
we may try to cover up and continue to testify, but there
is no power, no conviction. Our opponents may even say,

'Your actions speak so loud that I cannot hear what you say.'

PRAYER THAT I MAY TRIUMPH ONLY THROUGH HIM

verse 44: **So shall I keep** *Your law continually,*
Forever and ever.

The verse begins with *vav*, which may be translated in a variety of ways as well as 'and'. Here the New King James Version (following the Authorized Version) has translated it 'so'. 'Nothing more effectually binds a man to the way of the Lord than an experience of the truth of his word, embodied in the form of mercies and deliverances. Not only does the Lord's faithfulness open our mouths against his adversaries, but it also knits our hearts to his fear, and makes our union with Him more and more intense. ... God's grace alone can enable us to keep his commandments without break and without end' [13]. So, because He strengthens and revives and enables us, we can keep His law in the form of Christ's commandments for us today.

A PROMISE: PERFECT FREEDOM IS TO BE HIS SLAVE

verse 45: **And I will walk** *at liberty,*
For I seek Your precepts.

Am I stating a contradiction? Is to be His slave really perfect liberty? Yes, indeed. Ask all those who have totally submitted to His blessed will. What joy! What perfect liberty not to have to do our own will, as before, but His will. Free at last to do His will. Free from bondage to the will of the flesh, and free from self-will! 'For I seek Your precepts.' It is as we search the scriptures that we shall find this secret of perfect liberty. It is at the end of Romans chapter seven that we see a soul cry out in bitterness, 'O wretched man that I am! Who will deliver me from this body of death?' He is miserable, because he is under the tyranny of sin and self. But he discovers the secret, 'I thank God—through Jesus Christ our Lord!' Have we yielded to the Lordship of Christ yet?

A PROMISE: MY LIPS ARE HIS

verse 46: **I will speak** *of Your testimonies also before kings,*
And will not be ashamed.

Delivered from the bondage and tyranny of sin and self, now we can yield to our new Master, the Lord Jesus Christ! There was a time, in our unregenerate days, when Psalm 12:2-4 might have been applicable to any one of us, '… with flattering lips and a double heart they speak. May the Lord cut off all flattering lips, and the tongue that speaks proud things, who have said, "With our tongue we will prevail; our lips are our own; who is lord over us?"' I hope that my reader can say, 'My lips are *His.*' What do we use our mouths and our lips for now? Surely our verse helps us, 'I will speak of Your testimonies also before kings, and will not be ashamed.' Think of how the apostle Paul stood before king Agrippa, before Festus and Felix, and gave a ringing testimony to his faith in the living God (Acts 26 etc).

A PROMISE: MY HEART IS HIS ALSO

verse 47: **And I will delight myself** *in Your commandments,*
Which I love.

It is a very good habit to have our hearts and thoughts occupied with the Lord and His word the moment we awake in the morning. Many believers know the joy of keeping a regular Quiet Time with the Lord and His word. Do you? It is not easy to find time each day for this. Many believers have totally disorganised lives, they wander aimlessly through each day and feel dissatisfied as they seem to accomplish nothing really positive. Do you feel like that? Have you organised your life? You will always recognise a spiritual and fruitful believer – his life-style is an organised life-style. 'My voice You shall hear in the morning, O LORD; in the morning I will direct it to You, and I will look up' (Psalm 5:3). Many men of God in the Bible 'arose early in the morning' to do what the Lord required of them. Of the Lord Jesus we read that 'in the morning, having risen a long while before daylight, ... He prayed' (Mark 1:35). This is indeed the secret of the victorious life, a life of prayer and study of the Word of God.

A PROMISE: MY HANDS AND MY BODY ARE HIS

verse 48:   *My hands **also I will lift up** to Your command-*
ments,
Which I love,
And I will meditate on Your statutes.

It is entirely appropriate that this section of eight verses should end with folded hands lifted up to the Lord in total dependence, relying on Him for victory in daily life. Nothing less than total surrender of our will to the Lord Jesus and submission to Him as His slaves, yielding our lips and our mouths and our hands to Him, is required so that we might realize His victory in our lives.

Division Three

VERSES 49-72
OUR IMMENSE SPIRITUAL RICHES

7. *Zain*   verses 49-56

   God's Word reveals our spiritual assets.

8. *Cheth*   verses 57-64

   God's Word transforms into His image.

9. *Teth*   verses 65-72

   God's Word strengthens in adversity.

ז

7. ZAIN – verses 49-56

Meaning: Weapon

Derivation: The shape of the letter resembles a hand-held weapon.

Numerical value: Seven (7)

Significance: It is the first letter of *zakar*, 'to remember' (compare the name 'Zachariah'; *zachar* – 'remembered', *iah* – 'of Jehovah'). What then does this letter suggest to us? Every Christian is given a weapon: 'the sword of the Spirit, which is the Word of God' (Ephesians 6:17); and that Word tells us of our immense spiritual riches. Remembering these, we are equipped for our spiritual warfare.

God's Word reveals our spiritual assets

PRECIOUS PROMISES

verse 49:   **Remember** *the word to Your servant,*
           Upon which You have caused me to hope.

It is the Psalmist who asks the Lord to remember His word! The Lord has given precious promises. Someone has tried to count all the promises given in the Bible and

70

has found more than 30,000 of them! Precious promises! We have this interesting word in Isaiah 62:6, 'You who make mention of the LORD, do not keep silent.' The best basis for prayer is the solid promises of God. Remind God of what He has said! 'The gifts and the calling of God are irrevocable' (Romans 11:29). 'As His divine power has given to us all things that pertain to life and godliness, through the knowledge of Him who called us by glory and virtue, by which have been given to us exceedingly great and precious promises, that through these you may be partakers of the divine nature …' (2 Peter 1:3-4). The Psalmist is saying in effect, 'This is the word and these are the promises upon which You have caused me to hope.' How wonderful that the Bible gives us hope in afflictions (verse 49), and comfort (verse 50), even in troubles (verses 51-53), and it gives joy (verses 54-56). God is always faithful to His promises!

POSSESSING OUR POSSESSIONS

verse 50:   ***This*** *is my comfort in my affliction,*
           For Your word has given me life.

The question is whether we have appropriated and do appropriate these exceeding great and precious promises! This appropriating is by faith: we thank the Lord for every promise the Holy Spirit brings before us in our daily reading. We see something similar in Romans 6:11 where Paul says, 'Likewise you also, *reckon* yourselves to be dead.' It is not the reckoning that makes the fact, but I am to reckon in view of the fact. I appropriate in view of the fact that every spiritual blessing in the heavenlies in Christ is put to my account by the Father. It is therefore in the appropriating that we experience the 'comfort in my affliction'. It is when we thank the Lord for His promises that we experience what the Psalmist affirms, 'for Your Word has given me life.' Notice, here is no prayer for deliverance *from* the affliction! But although the affliction remains, the comfort is there so that we may be able to bear it, and be victorious in it.

No PROMISES FOR THE PROUD

verse 51: **The proud** *have me in great derision,*
Yet I do not turn aside from Your law.

By the proud are meant the unbelievers! They cannot understand the quiet confidence of the believer and therefore ridicule him. Ridicule is a powerful weapon Satan uses against believers, to make them doubt the promises of God. But we should not be surprised by this ridicule. The apostle Paul tells us, 'All who desire to live godly in Christ Jesus will suffer persecution' (2 Timothy 3:12). The natural man does not receive, and cannot understand, the things of the Spirit of God, for they are foolishness to him (see 1 Corinthians 2:14). So let us arm ourselves! If the enemy seeks to make us doubt the promises of God, let us not give him one inch! It is the purpose of the enemy to make us 'turn aside from the law (the Word of God)', but with the Lord's help his efforts will only strengthen us, and make us more determined to trust the Lord and realize His promises.

REMEMBER!

verse 52: **I remembered** *Your judgments of old,*
O LORD, And have comforted myself.

We forget so quickly! In verse 49 he asked the Lord to remember His Word; here he remembers! It is like saying, 'let the Word of Christ dwell in you richly in all wisdom' (Colossians 3:16). There is no victory possible without that Word abiding in us. We must constantly use the 'sword of the Spirit, which is the Word of God' (Ephesians 6:17). We should learn practical lessons from Jehovah's 'judgments of old', when He dealt with His people Israel.

'Now all these things happened to them as examples, and they were written for our admonition, upon whom the ends of the ages have come' (1 Corinthians 10:11). In Romans 15:4 we read, 'For whatever things were written before were written for our learning, that we through the patience and comfort of the Scriptures might have hope.' This then is the comfort we read of in our verse!

PITY THE PERISHING WITHOUT PROMISES

verse 53: **Indignation** *has taken hold of me*
Because of the wicked, who forsake Your law.

No true believer can remain unmoved when he sees the crowds in the streets and cities of this world 'having no hope and without God'. Can we be so complacent with our own safety and the blessings we have received that we remain indifferent to the end of those who deliberately 'forsake Your law'? The word for indignation is better translated as the 'hot zeal' of compassion for these lost souls.

BELIEVERS HAVE REASON TO SING

verse 54: *Your statutes have been* **my songs**
In the house of my pilgrimage.

We do not have to wait till we get to heaven in order to sing! This verse speaks of our pilgrimage. 'He has put a new song in my mouth—praise to our God' (Psalm 40:3). We have indeed many reasons to be joyful and to sing on the way to the Father's house. Happy the heart that finds its joy in the statutes of God. Remember that statute means a divine direction to obtain our obedience. What joy there is in obeying Him!

BLESSED INSOMNIA!

verse 55: **I remember** *Your name in the night, O L*ORD*,*
And I keep Your law.

We all know periods in our spiritual experience which are comparable to nights, when things are dark and we are restless and long for the morning to dawn. Whether they are literal nights, and we suffer from real insomnia, or other kinds of nights, let us remember the Lord's *name.* The name stands for the Person. How many wonderful names does our heavenly Father have, and our blessed Lord and Master Jesus Christ. There are whole books written about the significances of these names! And every name brings comfort and encouragement. 'Those who know Your *name* will put their trust in You' (Psalm 9:10). 'The *name* of the LORD is a strong tower; the righteous run to it and are safe' (Proverbs 18:10). So the pilgrim is enabled by the Holy Spirit to sing along his pilgrim path day by day, and even in the night he can sing when he remembers what the Lord is to him.

LET US NOT LOSE WHAT WE HAVE

verse 56: **This** *has become mine,*
Because I kept Your precepts.

What is it he had? The comfort he has spoken of in the previous verses no doubt. Is he looking back now and saying, 'I had this once, but not now'? Is he speaking of a past experience? 'This I had, because I kept Thy precepts' (AV)! But here is a warning for us. Let us not lose what we have. We can have this sense of His presence daily, this comfort of His companionship on our pilgrim pathway, this joy in Him and in obeying Him. Let us not grieve the Lord or the Holy Spirit, but seek His fellowship. Then we shall discover our immense spiritual possessions!

ח

8. CHETH – verses 57-64

Meaning: Fence

Derivation: The shape of this letter in the Phoenician monuments and the Hebrew coins resembles a hedge, and therefore its name probably signifies a fence, cognate with the Arabic root *hat* to surround, to gird.

Numerical value: Eight (8)
                 This reminds us of resurrection.

Significance: We are reminded of the verse: "For You, O LORD, will bless the righteous; with favour You will surround him as with a shield" (Psalms 5:12). Fellowship is being fenced in with Him.

God's Word transforms into His image

I AM HIS AND HE IS MINE

verse 57:   ***You are my portion, O LORD;***
              I have said that I would keep Your words.

We had precious promises in the previous section. Here we have a precious portion. The Hebrew has literally 'My portion is Jahweh.' We are not talking about blessings, or promises, but about a Person now! Him! Many Christians are so occupied with the blessings that they forget the Blesser, and likewise many are so enthralled with their spiritual gifts, that they ignore the Giver! In the previous section the Psalmist counted his blessings, but here he revels in the vision of the Blesser. Psalm 73:25 expresses it beautifully, 'Whom have I in heaven?' ('but You' is added in many translations, but it is not in the original) 'and there is none upon earth that I desire besides You.'

HE IS GRACIOUS

verse 58:   ***I entreated*** *Your favour with my whole heart;*
               Be merciful to me according to Your word.

The literal meaning of the Hebrew word translated 'favour' is 'face'. He was longing for the very presence of the Lord. Again it is the Person who is the object here as in verse 57. Does not all this have a bearing on the very letter *cheth* above this section which stands for the intimacy of our being fenced in with Him? Does not all this speak of fellowship? The presence of the Lord is indeed the highest form of His favour. We often sing,

> *There is a light that shines on me,*
> *The light of Jesus' face,*
> *Oh, what a glory thus to be,*
> *The object of His grace.*

That about expresses what we have in this verse. His presence brings with it the favour we seek. The verse continues in the Hebrew, 'favour (or, be gracious to) me according to Your word.' Now this is a petition which the Christian need not pray. We do not have to ask God to be favourable to us, for He has abundantly shown His favour. Paul says, 'To the praise of the glory of His grace, by which He has made us accepted in the Beloved' (Ephesians 1:6). 'Through whom also we have access ...

into this grace in which we stand' (Romans 5:2). The Psalmist asks nothing beyond what God has revealed, 'according to Your word.'

TRANSFORMING MEDITATION

verse 59: **I thought** *about my ways,*
And turned my feet to Your testimonies.

In this verse we can all think back to how it was that God showed His mercy and grace to us in Christ and accepted us in Him. Let us follow the sequence:

a. 'I thought about my ways': the arrest and conviction of the Holy Spirit.

b. 'and turned my feet to Your testimonies': conversion – the sinner makes a complete turn, and judges his past.

c. The third step I shall consider in the next verse.

We must not stop at self-examination, though that is necessary in its time. But we turn to *Him,* the object of our faith and the bestower of grace and mercy. 'Ponder the path of your feet, and let all your ways be established' (Proverbs 4:26).

NEVER PROCRASTINATE!

verse 60: **I made haste,** *and did not delay*
To keep Your commandments.

To 'procrastinate' means to waste time, to defer action, to postpone. Continuing the sequence I started in verse 59:

c. 'I made haste, and did not delay to keep Your commandments.' Of course, a sinner cannot be saved by keeping His commandments, but in this sentence we find an important principle that forms part of a true conversion – total submission and capitulation to His word. There must be obedience to the word of repentance. Now, what is true at the beginning of our spiritual lives is also true for the continuation of them. Never put off till tomorrow what you must do today. Prompt obedience is the secret of true spiritual growth.

SATAN SEEKS TO ROB ME OF THE SENSE OF JESUS' PRESENCE

verse 61: **The cords** *of the wicked have bound me,*
But I have not forgotten Your law.

Here is an attempt made by the enemy to stop the progress of the believer. He uses all sorts of devices to this end. The world may rob me of my *joy* in the Lord Jesus Christ. Sin may rob me of the sense of His *presence* and peace. Satan seeks to hem me in, to surround me and cut me off from enjoying the fellowship and communion with the Lord Jesus. The apostle Paul says that we should not be ignorant of Satan's devices (2 Corinthians 2:11). The Lord Jesus says, 'Hold fast what you have, that no one may take your crown' (Revelation 3:11). Satan cannot make us lose our salvation, or eternal life, but he can rob us of much that makes up that crown. To counteract this strategy of the enemy, the believer should positively occupy himself with the Word of God. 'I have not forgotten Your law.'

BLESSED INSOMNIA! (SEE VERSE 55)

verse 62: At **mid**night I will rise to give thanks to You,
Because of Your righteous judgments.

When all is quiet at last, God can speak. Elihu knew about this when he said, 'For God may speak in one way, or in another, yet man does not perceive it. In a dream, in a vision of the night, when deep sleep falls upon men, while slumbering on their beds, then He opens the ears of men' (Job 33:14-16). Paul and Silas, 'at midnight … were praying and singing hymns to God, and the prisoners were listening to them' (Acts 16:25). Of king Ahasuerus we read, 'That night the king could not sleep' (Esther 6:1). Then things were brought to his notice which he had previously ignored, and consequently he set matters straight. So insomnia, or sleeplessness, can sometimes be a hidden blessing. In any case, it is always a good habit when we suffer from sleeplessness to praise and pray. 'I will rise to give thanks to You.'

MAKE FRIENDS OF GOD'S CHILDREN

*verse 63:   I am **a companion** of all who fear You,*
*   And of those who keep Your precepts.*

It has sometimes been said, 'Show me your friends, and I will tell you who you are.' The Bible gives this warning, 'Do not be deceived: "Evil company corrupts good habits"' (1 Corinthians 15:33). Proverbs 18:24 (NIV) has this precious encouragement, 'A man of many companions may come to ruin, but there is a friend who sticks closer than a brother.' Let us attach ourselves to that Friend. What a Friend we have in the Lord Jesus! As we seek the fellowship of the Lord Jesus, remembering that the theme of this section of eight verses is fellowship, we shall also seek the companionship of all those that fear Him. How can two walk together unless they are agreed (Amos 3:3)?

THE TRANSFORMING VISION

*verse 64:   The earth, O LORD, is full of **Your mercy**;*
*   Teach me Your statutes.*

This section began with the emphasis on mercy and favour (verse 58), and now it rightly finishes with the same thought. How we need His continuing mercy day by day. Grace is seen in that He gives us what we do not deserve; mercy is seen in that He does not give us what we do deserve. *He* therefore fills our vision from the beginning to the end of this section of eight verses. It is a transforming vision! He is my portion; He is so gracious; He is my Friend. Indeed, 'the earth is full of Your mercy.'

מ

9. TETH - verses 65-72

Meaning:	Snake or Coil
Derivation:	The meaning of this letter is uncertain. It is generally thought to signify a serpent (Arabic *tet*), to which its shape has a resemblance in several Phoenicio-Semitic alphabets. Others make it something like 'rolled or twisted together', similar to the Arabic root *tih*, or perhaps it is the Egyptian *tôt*, hand.

Numerical value: Nine (9)

Significance:	A snake reminds us of 'that serpent of old, called the Devil and Satan, who deceives the whole world' (Revelation 12:9).

God's Word strengthens in adversity

LET'S COUNT OUR BLESSINGS!

verse 65: *You have dealt **well** with Your servant, O LORD, according to Your word.*

'Good You have done with Your servant', is the literal rendering in Hebrew. When you feel depressed, count your blessings! We often sing that hymn,

> *Count your blessings, name them one by one,*
> *and it will surprise you what the Lord has done.*

This is an excellent therapy for discouragements. In verse 67 he speaks of having been afflicted. He has learned that even when the Lord deals with us in discipline we can give thanks and say afterwards, 'You have dealt well with Your servant.' Jacob saw this in his experience. In Genesis 42:36 he says, 'All these things are against me.' In chapter 45:27, 'the spirit of Jacob their father revived', and in chapter 48:15, 'God, before whom my fathers Abraham and Isaac walked, the God who has fed me all my life long to this day.' Jacob realises that 'nevertheless, afterward it yields the peaceable fruit of righteousness' (Hebrews 12:11). This verse is an answer to the prayer the Psalmist prayed in verse 17, 'Deal bountifully with Your servant', 'You have dealt well with Your servant.' Can you look back and thank the Lord for everything?

GOOD MAY BE THE ENEMY OF THE BEST

*verse 66: Teach me **good** judgment and knowledge,*
For I believe Your commandments.

He prays for discernment or judgment. The root meaning of the word translated 'judgment' is 'taste'; and here it is used of the spiritual sense of taste for judgment, discernment, reason. Paul prays for the Philippians in chapter one verse 10, ' That you may approve the things that are excellent' or, as the NIV puts it, 'so that you may be able to discern what is best'. For the believer it is not only a question of refusing sin or sinful things, but of discerning what is profitable and constructive, and what is not. Good judgment and knowledge are essential for spiritual growth. Hebrews 5:14, 'But solid food belongs to those who are of full age, that is, those who by reason of use have their senses exercised to discern both good and evil.'

Now this kind of spiritual discernment does not come to us automatically, as we learn from the verse in Hebrews 5. It comes with practice. That is why the writer begins this verse 66 with, 'Teach me.' Are we willing to be taught?

DISCIPLINE RESULTS IN EXPERIENCE

verse 67: **Before** *I was afflicted I went astray,*
But now I keep Your word.

God has been dealing with him (verse 65), and now he can give thanks! Let us take encouragement from these words in Proverbs 3:11-12, 'My son, do not despise the chastening of the LORD, nor detest His correction; for whom the LORD loves He corrects, just as a father the son in whom he delights.' How many parents there are today, even Christian parents, who do not discipline their children according to the Scriptures. They think that it is unkind to punish a child and to correct it, or to give it corporal punishment when necessary. This is of course Freudian psychology, but not Biblical instruction. In fact, it is a lack of love that does not correct and guide a child when it goes wrong, or when it must be compelled for its own sake. The result of the discipline the Psalmist had accepted was that he could say, 'Now I keep Your word.' Had there previously been resistance, or rebelliousness on his part? The necessary discipline that had followed had brought forth that peaceable fruit of righteousness, and for this he is thankful. Can we thank the Lord for discipline?

ALL THINGS WORK TOGETHER FOR GOOD

verse 68: *You* **are good***, and do good;*
Teach me Your statutes.

God can never do anything that is not good and beneficent! He is good in His essential nature, and therefore whatever He does must be good! Do we doubt this?

Romans 8:28 gives us these wonderful facts about God's unfailing purpose:

a.   all things work together for *good* – beneficent.
b.   all things *work* together for good – active.
c.   *all things* work together for good – inclusive.
d.   all things *work together* for good – harmonious.

It is God's purpose to conform us to the image of His Son. His discipline in our lives has this one aim: to make us more and more like His Son.

EVIL IS ALWAYS PLOTTING

verse 69:   *The proud **have forged** a lie against me,*
           But I will keep Your precepts with my whole heart.

Here we have the first mention of the adversary. It is in connection with verses 69 and 70 that we see the need for the enabling of the Word of God by strengthening us in adversity, as the title of this section pointed out. Satan is called 'the accuser of our brethren' (Revelation 12:10), as well as 'a liar and the father of it' (John 8:44). Those who are his children, of course, bear the same characteristics and are said in this verse to 'have forged a lie' against the godly man. Let us never be surprised when this happens to us. However, if they are occupied with 'forging lies', let us who love the truth be occupied with the Word of God. The verse here helps us as it continues, 'I will keep Your precepts with my whole heart.'

SPIRITUAL CHOLESTEROL KILLS!

verse 70:   *Their heart **is as fat** as grease,*
           But I delight in Your law.

'Without feeling, like fat, is their heart', is the literal translation. A fat heart is a slow heart that might finally be brought to a halt and die. Cholesterol is a killer for the body as well as for the spirit! Believers are certainly not children of the evil one, but unfortunately they may sometimes be like the unregenerate in their behaviour. For instance, there are believers who are never on time, who are always late at the meetings for prayer or Bible-study or edification or worship! Do you know them? They lack spiritual energy. It seems that the round of meetings is a real burden to them. They go through the motions, but their heart is not in it. They need our prayer that they may be revived and energised and healed from their spiritual fat heart. May we be characterised by a fervent spirit, serving the Lord whole-heartedly!

THE HIDDEN BLESSINGS OF AFFLICTION

verse 71:   **It is good** *for me that I have been afflicted,*
              That I may learn Your statutes.

The writer to the Hebrews tell us, 'Now no chastening seems to be joyful for the present, but painful; nevertheless, afterward it yields the peaceable fruit of righteousness to those who have been trained by it' (chapter 12:11). This is not easy to accept, especially when we are actually going through a trying period in our lives. The apostle Paul had learned to glory in his infirmities! He could say that when he felt utterly weak, then he was made strong by the strength of the Lord. And so it always is. The Psalmist also sees the positive side of affliction, 'that I may learn Your statutes.' Nothing is lost in the school of faith in which we are all enrolled as believers. And this thought leads me to the last verse of this section:

THERE IS NO GAIN BUT BY A LOSS

verse 72:   *The law of Your mouth* **is better** *to me*
              Than thousands of coins of gold and silver.

To say 'There is no gain but by a loss', means that in order to gain spiritually we must be willing to lose first. This

85

principle is explained by the apostle Paul in the Letter to the Philippians, 'But what things were gain to me, these I have counted loss for Christ. Yet indeed I also count all things loss for the excellence of the knowledge of Christ Jesus my Lord, for whom I have suffered the loss of all things, and count them as rubbish, that I may gain Christ' (chapter 3:7-8).

In verse 72 we have contrasted thousands of gold and silver coins on the one hand, and the law of Your mouth on the other. The Psalmist chooses the law, i.e. the Word of God. What do we choose? Remember in the Introduction I said that the meaning of the word 'Law' is a divine instruction concerning our conduct and our character. It comes from the verb meaning to throw, show, teach or instruct. The writer would sacrifice anything, like gold or silver, if only he might have the guidance of God in his life, if only he may know the will of the Lord for every step of the way! I summarise this section as follows:

verse 65:   What God *does* is good;

verse 66:   What God *teaches* is good;

verse 67:   When God *afflicts* it is for our good;

verse 68:   God *is* good;

verse 72:   God's *word* is good.

To know this is the best armour for the fight in a day of adversity and opposition.

Division Four

VERSES 73-96
SPIRITUAL MATURITY THROUGH DAILY MEDITATION

10. *Yod*   verses 73-80

    God's Word shows us our responsibility.

11. *Kaph*   verses 81-88

    God's Word for our security.

12. *Lamed*   verses 89-96

    God's Word helps us mature spiritually.

י

10. YOD – verses 73-80

Meaning: Hand

Derivation: Without any doubt, the meaning of this letter is 'hand'. In Phoenician and Samaritan writing, as well as on the coins of the Maccabees, this letter presents the figure of a hand crudely drawn. In the Ethiopic language it has the name of *yaman*, i.e. right hand. The letter is called *yod* from the Hebrew word *yad* which means hand. This is seen in the shape of the letter which looks like a hand pointing from right to left. Hebrew is written from right to left like Arabic.

Numerical value: Ten (10)

Significance: The *yod* is also the smallest letter of the Hebrew alphabet. In the Greek the letter *iota* (which is printed the same way as the English 'i' except it has no dot) is also the smallest letter. Do we not have an important lesson here to remember? The hand of man, man himself, is so very insignificant in spite of all his boastfulness. Nevertheless, with ten fingers on his hand, and ten toes on his feet, he is responsible to God. We have then the idea of responsibility in this letter. We all remember what the Lord Jesus said in Matthew 5:18, 'For assuredly, I say to you, till heaven and earth pass away, one jot or one tittle will by no means pass from the law till all is fulfilled.' The Lord was referring to the letter *yod* of the Hebrew alphabet, which, when written in Greek is *iota* and has become jot in our Bibles. The letter *yod* is spelt in Hebrew simply *yd* – *daleth-yod* reading from right to left. We have already learned that *daleth* means 'door'. So the two letters together spell this thought: a hand is pointing to the door. The Lord Jesus is the door into salvation for poor sinners (John 10:9).

God's Word shows us our responsibility

NO EVOLUTION, BUT CREATION!

verse 73: **Your hands** *have made me and fashioned me; Give me understanding, that I may learn Your commandments.*

In Isaiah 43:6-7 we read, 'Bring My sons from afar, and My daughters from the ends of the earth—everyone who is called by My name, whom I have created for My glory; I have formed him, yes, I have made him.' It is clear from this that the Bible teaches creation, not evolution.

a. As to our *spirit*, God says, I have *created* him;
b. As to our *body*, God says, I have *formed* him;
c. As to our *soul*, God says, I have *made* him.

Job adds to this, 'Your hands have made me and fashioned me, an intricate unity; yet You would destroy me' (10:8). Let God be true, and every man a liar. Let me study the circulatory system, plasma, the nervous system, the brain and indeed the eye. 'Give me understanding', and I will know that God created me, and that I am a responsible intelligent human being answerable to Him.

THOSE WHO ARE GENUINE

verse 74: **Those who fear** *You will be glad when they see me,*
Because I have hoped in Your word.

Here we have the encouraging influence of a tried but steadfast believer. Others can see how he has come through trials, and perhaps intellectual doubts and he becomes to them a source of gladness. The apostle Paul speaks of this in Philippians 1:14, 'Most of the brethren in the Lord, having become confident by my chains, are much more bold to speak the word without fear.' They had seen how Paul could rejoice in the midst of persecution and trials, and how he had hoped in the word of the Lord. How do others see you and me? What kind of an example or influence are we in our surroundings? Whether we are conscious of it or not, we are an influence for good or for bad. We are therefore forcibly reminded of our individual responsibility to be a help and blessing and not a hindrance. If we are genuine and sensitive to the Holy Spirit's guidance, we shall be an encouragement to many.

WE MUST BE POSITIVE

verse 75: **I know**, *O* LORD, *that Your judgments are right,*
And that in faithfulness You have afflicted me.

Speaking about being an influence for good in our surroundings, here we have it more precisely expressed in the way I have headed this verse – we must be positive! Negative influences are destructive and a hindrance to the progress of the saints. First, we must be positive in our attitude towards the Lord and the ways in which He deals with us: 'In faithfulness You have afflicted me.' How emphatic the writer is, 'I know, O LORD, that Your judgments are right.' What He decides is for our good! Once we are sure that His way is best for us, we can accept it and be happy in it. Think of Paul again in prison writing to the Philippians (chapter 1:14). Satan is baffled by such believers! He cannot handle that kind of attitude!

Now follow five 'lets'.

LET HIS KINDNESS ENFOLD YOU

verse 76: **Let,** *I pray, Your merciful kindness* **be** *for my comfort,*
According to Your word to Your servant.

The Lord gives grace and helps in time of need. When we need strength and enabling for the tasks He gives us, His grace is abundant. However, should we fail, or come short, then His mercy is there to lift us up. He restores and set us upon our feet and encourages us to start again! Like the Psalmist we can pray this prayer, '*Let Your merciful kindness be for my comfort.*' We are so vulnerable, so frail, so weak, so insignificant! He knows our frailty and that is why we need Him to enfold us in His arms. What comfort to a little child it is to be enfolded in his mother's arms after he has fallen.

LET HIS MERCY COMFORT YOU

verse 77: **Let** *Your tender mercies* **come to me,** *that I may live;*
For Your law is my delight.

Here a visitor is invited who is expected to bring what we so desperately need at the moment. There has been failure. I have failed in my responsibility. I am conscious of defeat and am discouraged. I hesitate to come to Him, but He is already on the way to me to lift me up and comfort me. Notice He brings tender mercies! Let me quote the words of a saint, 'The mercies of God are "tender mercies", they are the mercies of a father to his children, nay, tender as the compassion of a mother over the son of her womb. They "come unto" us, when we are not able to go to them. By them alone we "live" the life of faith, of love, of joy and gladness. And to such as "delight" in His law, God will grant these mercies and this life; He will give them pardon, and, by so doing, He will give them life from the dead' [8].

LET HIM KEEP ME HUMBLE

verse 78: **Let** *the proud* **be ashamed,**
For they treated me wrongfully with falsehood;
But I will meditate on Your precepts.

Let me repeat this question once more: What kind of people are we? What kind of impression do we give to others? What kind of influence do we spread around us? Positive? Are we like the Lord Jesus? Or are we rather superior, rather haughty, rather obnoxious? Do we give others cause to oppose us in any way? The Lord Jesus Christ could say, 'They hated Me without a cause' (John 15:25; see Psalm 35:19; 69:4). How then could the proud who 'treated me wrongfully with falsehood' be made ashamed? Surely, when they find no real reason to criticise or condemn us for anything inconsistent, or anything repugnant in our lives. When they see our good works they must give glory to God! 'Let your light so shine before men, that they may see your good works and glorify your Father in heaven' (Matthew 5:16).

Let His winsomeness clothe me

verse 79: **Let** *those who fear You* **turn to me,**
Those who know Your testimonies.

This certainly is a Christ-honouring prayer! We do not seek to attract people to ourselves, but to our Lord Jesus. But our lives must therefore be winsome. This winsomeness is what the early Christians displayed at Jerusalem: 'having favour with all the people' (Acts 2:47). There are believers whose lives are upright, whose doctrine is absolutely correct and transparent like ice, but sometimes unfortunately just as cold. It is a cold kind of correctness; there is very little that is warm or attractive about them. Not so these Spirit-filled believers at Jerusalem. We are responsible to proclaim Christ by our lips and by our lives. He should be manifested in our lives, and that is what makes others who 'fear Him turn to us', and walk in fellowship with us.

Let my heart be true

verse 80: **Let** *my heart be* **blameless regarding Your**
statutes,
That I may not be ashamed.

This seems to be the key verse of this section. What a prayer this is! There are the proud liars in verse 78. Yet might there not be a measure of hypocrisy in any one of us? Pretending to be so pious and spiritual on the outside, yet not totally yielded to the Lord Jesus? It is only when the Holy Spirit fills us and directs and guides us that we shall be kept blameless and not be ashamed before our own consciences, nor ashamed before the world's scrutiny, nor one day ashamed before the judgment seat of Christ.

כ

11. KAPH - verses 81-88

Meaning: The Palm of the Hand

Derivation: This eleventh letter of the alphabet signifies a wing or it may also signify the
hollow of the hand, i.e. palm. Its form
in the Hebrew alphabet is like the curve
of the hand between the forefinger and
the thumb: representing the palm of the
hand.

Numerical value: Twenty (20)

Hebrew usage: When it is prefixed to a word, it means
as, like, as if, according to (a number of
times in Psalm 119) or when. (This is
similar to Arabic.)

Significance: It will not be far-fetched to suggest that
we have here the idea of security; in
Isaiah 49:16 we read, 'See, I have
inscribed you on the palms of My
hands; your walls are continually before
Me.' In the palms of His hands we are
secure!

God's Word for our security

ONLY HE CAN REALLY SATISFY

verse 81:   *My soul **faints** for Your salvation,*
                But I hope in Your word.

This whole section speaks of danger from enemies! Verse 81 '*My soul faints*'; verse 83 '*I have become like a wineskin in smoke*'; verse 84 '*those who persecute me*'; verse 85 '*The proud have dug pits for me*'; verse 86 '*They persecute me*'; verse 87 '*They almost made an end of me*'. Conscious of being under attack from the enemy, the writer seeks refuge with the Lord and His Word. His only hope is in the Lord, and so it is for you and me. We cannot help ourselves, nor can anyone else help us, which is why we have this pathetic cry, 'My soul faints for Your salvation.' It is good to realise day by day what we sometimes sing in a hymn: '*Now none but Christ can satisfy.*' Have we found this secret yet?

WE MAY FAIL, HE NEVER WILL

verse 82:   *My eyes **fail** from searching Your word,*
                Saying, "When will You comfort me?"

Do we discern a note of impatience? '*When will You comfort me?*' Had he not been hoping in His word (verse 81)? Why does not the Lord act quickly? 'Hope deferred makes the heart sick' (Proverbs 13:12). Do not let yourself be discouraged by appearances. Peter said, 'The Lord is not slack concerning His promise' (2 Peter 3:9). We sometimes want to limit the Lord to our time. Sometimes we cannot see the reason for such and such a thing. But we should leave everything in His hands. He is never too late. We must learn to persevere in faith and hope and the study of His word, and take our eyes off our circumstances.

I AM NOTHING

verse 83: **For** *I have become like a wineskin in smoke,*
Yet I do not forget Your statutes.

He is really exhausted. The strain and stress have been unbearable. Of course Satan's strategy is to wear us out! It was by the constant nagging of Delilah that Samson's soul was 'vexed to death' (Judges 16:16). She wore him out. It is necessary for us to get to this end of ourselves, to despair of our own self-sufficiency. When we get to the end of our own resources, then we realise that our Father's full giving is only just begun. When we feel empty, and our spiritual energy seems shrivelled up like a wineskin in smoke, when we realise our own nothingness, then we are ready for His fulness to be revealed on our behalf. How do you see yourself?

I FEEL HAUNTED

verse 84: **How many** *are the days of Your servant?*
When will You execute judgment on those who
persecute me?

'How?' 'When?' He is so full of questions in this verse. Is he complaining? He certainly seems impatient. Does he say, 'Lord, when are You going to deal with these ene-mies?' Of course it is not Christian to ask for the execution of our enemies; rather we should pray for their salvation. However, let us not forget that Psalm 119 gives us the expressions of the Faithful Remnant of Israel dur-ing the Great Tribulation. We can understand therefore that they are wondering when the Lord will come to deliver them. Our enemies are not of flesh and blood, but wicked spirits of darkness and spiritual powers. The day of their judgment is certainly getting near and they know it. That is why we see in our days such a world-wide mani-festation of occult and demonic powers. Yes, we are under attack. Yes, we are engaged in a spiritual warfare, and therefore should put on the whole armour of God, and resist, having done all, to stand, and not fail or falter. The Lord is our strength and our security.

THE BATTLE CONTINUES

verse 85: *The proud **have dug** pits for me,*
Which is not according to Your law.

Paul tells us in 2 Thessalonians 1:6, 'It is a righteous thing with God to repay with tribulation those who trouble you.' But that moment has not yet come for the New Testament believer waiting for the Coming of the Lord Jesus. For the moment we must accept what the Lord Jesus said: 'In the world you will have tribulation; but be of good cheer, I have overcome the world' (John 16:33). The apostle Peter says, 'Beloved, do not think it strange concerning the fiery trial which is to try you, as though some strange thing happened to you; but rejoice to the extent that you partake of Christ's sufferings, that when His glory is revealed, you may also be glad with exceeding joy' (1 Peter 4:12-13).

ALL WHO DESIRE TO LIVE GODLY WILL SUFFER PERSECUTION

verse 86: ***All** Your commandments are faithful;*
They persecute me wrongfully;
Help me!

It is good to remind ourselves that His word and His promises are faithful. It is commendable to suffer persecution because we want to remain faithful to Him and His word. Is this our intention and determination? The quotation at the head of this verse (2 Timothy 3:12), was written by the apostle Paul to Timothy. In this verse we have:

a. The *intention* to live godly: 'All who *desire to* live godly'
b. The *secret* power for godly living: '*in Christ Jesus*'
c. The *cost* of godly living: 'will suffer *persecution*'.

ACCOUNTED AS SHEEP FOR THE SLAUGHTER

verse 87:   *They **almost** made an end of me on earth,*
          But I did not forsake Your precepts.

Yes, even believers are not spared any tribulations or any sufferings. No doubt, when you or I are passing through a very difficult circumstance, Satan may insinuate that the Lord has forgotten us, and that He does not love us any more. The apostle Paul gives us some help on those circumstances when he writes to the believers at Rome who were also being persecuted. 'Who shall separate us from the love of Christ? Shall tribulation, or distress, or persecution, or famine, or nakedness, or peril, or sword? ... Yet in all these things we are more than conquerors through Him who loved us' (Romans 8:35, 37). Satan may use circumstances to sow doubts in our hearts. But why should we doubt? Is not God for us? Did not God give up His Son for us? Did not God justify us? Did not Christ die for us? And does not the Lord Jesus always intercede for us? We have nothing to fear. We are absolutely secure.

MORE THAN CONQUERORS

verse 88:   *Revive me **according to Your lovingkindness**,*
          So that I may keep the testimony of Your mouth.

'For I am persuaded that neither death nor life, nor angels nor principalities nor powers, nor things present nor things to come, nor height nor depth, nor any other created thing, shall be able to separate us from the love of God which is in Christ Jesus our Lord' (Romans 8:38-39). What does it mean to be 'more than conquerors'? I quote from the writings of another: 'It may be that we do not "conquer" at all, but we do more: we wrest from defeat values that could never be gained by "conquest". Enduring tribulation, we gain hope which is not put to shame. Bearing persecution, we are demonstrating the meaning of true godliness. Suffering hunger, we are proving that man does not live by bread alone, but this is only possible "through Him that loved us" – through His grace' [10]. Jesus 'was crucified in weakness' (2 Corinthians 13:4) and yet the Cross released the greatest power to save!

ל

12. LAMED - verses 89-96

Meaning: Ox-Goad

Derivation: The name of this letter has the same meaning as *malmed*, an ox-goad. This is the form this letter has on the Phoenician monuments.

Numerical value: Thirty (30)
This letter has therefore the significance of 'teaching us to go on to maturity'.

Hebrew usage: It also has various other meanings when prefixed to other words. Then it means: to, towards, unto, even to, into, as to, with regard to, on account of, concerning, about, of, on behalf of, for, belonging to, etc. A tremendously versatile letter indeed!

Significance: An ox-goad is a stick with a sharp point, by which the ox is directed. All the above meanings I have given indicate giving direction. It is in teaching that the teacher gives direction to the pupil. The Talmud, which is a book of Jewish traditional teaching, means instruction. In Talmud, you can see the three consonants of *lamed*.

God's Word helps us to mature spiritually

WE ARE SURE OF HIM AND HIS WORD

verse 89: **Forever, O LORD,**
Your word is settled in heaven.

In the first three verses we find words that indicate stability: settled (verse 89), established (verse 90) and continue (verse 91). Growing in the knowledge of God and His will gives stability to our walk. We must 'go on to maturity' (Hebrews 6:1, NIV) in our spiritual lives, and for this the Word is our daily food. 'Your Word is settled', and that Word settles the believer and makes him steadfast. Today the Word of God is under attack and so is the believer who believes it to be the absolute standard for his daily behaviour and conduct. Are we convinced that the Bible is indeed the breathing of God, God speaking to us, His inspired Word? The Bible is an incomparable and unique Book. Dear friends, read it, study it, meditate upon it, memorise it, ruminate on it, and you will grow in spiritual maturity.

JESUS NEVER FAILS

verse 90: *Your faithfulness **endures to all generations;***
You established the earth, and it abides.

In verse 89, the writer is convinced of the certainty of God's Word from the endurance of the heavens. Now he assures us of the same from his consideration of the foundation of the earth. The New Testament tells us concerning the blessed Person of the Lord Jesus Christ that He is 'the same yesterday, today, and forever' (Hebrews 13:8). The Lord Jesus has said, 'Heaven and earth will pass away, but My words will by no means pass away' (Matthew 24:35). This is the solid rock on which

101

we stand, the right foundation for our spiritual maturity. Nothing can shake either the Person of the Lord or His precious Word. 'You founded the earth and it still stands' is the literal rendering from the Hebrew. What God does endures! Someone said, 'Every time you set your foot on the ground remember the stability of God's promises' [9]. This is a useful way of continuing on our pathway to maturity.

IF ALL ARE HIS SERVANTS, WHY NOT ME?

verse 91:   *They continue this day **according to Your ordinances**,*
For all are Your servants.

'They continue this day' is the translation here. The NIV strangely says, 'Your laws endure to this day, for all things serve you.' But this is surely not the meaning. The 'they' in our verse are no doubt the 'word' in verse 89, and 'the earth' in verse 90! It is these: word, heaven and earth which are all His servants! If the Lord maintains and sustains these inanimate things, is He not able to sustain us? But also if the earth, heaven, the universe, hail, rain, the storm, the wind, the lightning, the thunder and the snow are all His servants, then how much more should you and I as redeemed and intelligent creatures be His servants. These elements function in their appointed place 'according to Your ordinances (or, judgments)' and are in this way an example to us all as members of the Body of Christ. We also have a special place where God has set us in the Body of Christ in order to function according to His will. Are we conscious of this and ready to fulfil our functions?

A CRISIS SHOWS WHAT WE REALLY ARE

verse 92:   **Unless** *Your law had been my delight,*
       I would then have perished in my affliction.

The Psalmist had been through some affliction and come through. He therefore speaks from experience and looks back with gratitude. It was the Word that had sustained him in those trying circumstances. How different is the experience of the Psalmist from that case described by the Lord Jesus in the parable of the sower, '... those who, when they have heard, go out and are choked with cares, riches, and pleasures of life, and bring no fruit to maturity' (Luke 8:14). Circumstances may show up our superficialities or, on the other hand, demonstrate that we are rooted and grounded in Him and His Word. Let us then daily delight in the reading and study of His Word.

LET US REMEMBER!

verse 93:   **I will never** *forget Your precepts,*
       For by them You have given me life.

When once we have experienced the truth of the Word of God in a particular circumstance or trial, we never forget it! Never to forget is also a very good resolution to make! Another thing he never forgot was that, when he passed through his trial and was so conscious of his own weakness, the Lord had revived him. It is through the Word of God that we get this reviving in our spirits. '... to be strengthened with might through His Spirit in the inner man' (Ephesians 3:16). His words are spirit and life (John 6:63), and His words are 'words of eternal life' (John 6:68).

I AM NOT MY OWN, BUT HIS!

verse 94:   **I am Yours***, save me;*
          For I have sought Your precepts.

He does not say: '*Save me, and I shall be Yours*', but he asserts that he belongs to the Lord and needs saving still! The Hebrew is emphatic here, 'Yours I am!' We used to sing in our youth,

> *Jesus saves me now,*
> *Jesus saves me now,*
> *Yes, Jesus saves me all the time,*
> *Jesus saves me now!*

Perhaps you ask how we can keep on asking to be saved when we have already been saved? The Psalmist says, 'I am Yours, save me; for I have sought Your precepts.' Of course the Old Testament saint knew nothing of what has been revealed to New Testament believers concerning the redemption of our bodies. They knew about soul/spirit salvation, but not about glorified bodies! Paul describes this final salvation in chapter eight of the Letter to the Romans, 'we … (are) eagerly waiting for the adoption, the redemption of our body' (verse 23). Peter calls this the 'salvation ready to be revealed in the last time' (1 Peter 1:5). Salvation therefore is a term which has a large meaning. There is salvation from or out of circumstances. This is what Paul refers to in Philippians 1:19, 'For I know that this will turn out for my deliverance (or, salvation) through your prayer and the supply of the Spirit of Jesus Christ.' Peter contrasts temporal deliverances in their circumstances with the salvation of the soul, when he says, 'Receiving the end of your faith—the salvation of your souls' (1 Peter 1:9).

WHAT CAN MEN DO TO ME?

verse 95: *The wicked **wait for me** to destroy me,*
But I will consider Your testimonies.

Here we have a practical example of the salvation from circumstances we have been talking about in the previous verse. Here is the enemy – 'The wicked wait for me to destroy me.' Certainly the Psalmist was looking to the Lord for salvation. But this had nothing to do with his soul's salvation. Satan has a well-developed strategy which he has acquired over thousands of years as an active adversary and tempter of the saints. He and his servants, the demons, often have to withdraw temporarily from their victim but will renew their attack at a more strategic moment – 'they wait for me to destroy me.' Let us not be deceived! If for the moment we have some respite from his attack, this is only a temporary lull in the battle, to make us relax. How do we overcome the powers of darkness? 'I write to you, young men, because you have overcome the wicked one. ... I have written to you ... because you are strong, and the word of God abides in you, and you have overcome the wicked one' (1 John 2:13-14). These verses give us the secret; we can only overcome the enemy through the Word of God when that word is living in us and we live by it every day. If this is true of you and me then we can say in the words of Hebrews 13:6, 'The LORD is my helper; I will not fear. What can man (or devil, or demon) do to me?'

OH, THE WIDENESS OF GOD'S MERCY!

verse 96: *I have seen the consummation **of all** perfection,*
But Your commandment is exceedingly broad.

To everything here on earth there is a limit, an end. Even the best of men do still sin. Even the most perfect in this world still fall far short of God's perfection. That is why the Psalmist has to say, 'I have seen an end of all perfection' (N.Tr.). There is no end even to our growing into spiritual maturity, and knowing Him! He is the infinite, we are finite. Paul had this desire to know Him, '… that I may know Him and the power of His resurrection, and the fellowship of His sufferings, being conformed to His death' (Philippians 3:10). The apostle John writes to the fathers, 'you have known Him who is from the beginning' (1 John 2:13-14). He repeats this statement twice because there really is no end to knowing Him. But they had grown from little children, to young men and now they were fathers. Here was indeed a growing into spiritual maturity. 'Your commandment is exceedingly broad', continues the writer. It is the same when we climb a high mountain; the higher we get, the more the view increases. At the top the panorama is breathtaking! So it is with the Word of God. It is an inexhaustible ocean of grace and wonders, a mine of jewels. There is no limit to the amount of confidence we can put in the Lord Jesus and His precious Word! 'Let us go on to perfection' (Hebrews 6:1), and to spiritual maturity.

Division Five

VERSES 97-120
THE IMPORTANCE OF DAILY BIBLE STUDY

13. *Mem*   verses 97-104

    God's Word is living water.

14. *Nun*   verses 105-112

    God's Word gives direction.

15. *Samech* verses 113-120

    God's Word for our support.

מ

13. MEM - verses 97-104

Meaning: Water

Derivation: Some suggest this letter looks like a
                    wave, from which it gets its name
                    'water'.

Numerical value: Forty (40)

Significance: Both God's Word and water were part
                    of His provision for Israel in the wilder-
                    ness: 'You also gave Your good Spirit to
                    instruct them, … and gave them water
                    for their thirst. Forty years You sus-
                    tained them in the wilderness'
                    (Nehemiah 9:20-21). In the New
                    Testament the connection between
                    water and the Word of God is clearly
                    established in Ephesians 5:26, where
                    the work of the Lord Jesus to 'sanctify
                    and cleanse' the Church is described as
                    'with the washing of water by the word';
                    and, to each believer, there is Jesus'
                    promise that 'He who believes in Me, as
                    the Scripture has said, out of his heart
                    will flow rivers of living water' (John
                    7:38).

God's Word is living water

THIRST FOR THE LIVING WORD

verse 97: **Oh, how** *I love Your law!*
It is my meditation all the day.

The Bible for Christians is the word of God. It is for us the standard to which we refer. We do not test the Bible by our experience but we test our experience by the Bible. Have you noticed how the writer of this Psalm is continually referring to the Word in its several aspects? It does seem that he knew his Bible as far as it was then revealed and written down. Do you know your Bible? For the Psalmist the Word of God was the final word. Is it for you my dear reader? Liberal theologians have the audacity to doubt many passages of the Bible and to undermine its authority. There is no doubt that, in order for the Christian to be strong spiritually, he simply *must* study the Bible. He must decide to set aside time for this study, just as he is willing to set aside time for any project he really wants to do. Do you always carry a copy of the Word with you? Not necessarily your study Bible, but a small pocket edition, so you have it handy when you are asked questions about your Christianity? When you reason with anyone, do you base what you say on the Scriptures? What a wonderful verse this is in fact. Let us read it again together: 'Oh, how I love Your law! It is my meditation all the day.'

THE BIBLE IS OUR ABSOLUTE STANDARD FOR CONDUCT

verse 98: *You, through Your commandments, make me*
*wiser **than my enemies**;*
For they are ever with me.

The Bible has always been under attack from the enemy of our souls. We are under attack as Christians today and are being continually challenged about our faith in that 'old-fashioned book'! I want you to be sure of this, it is not intellectual suicide to believe in the Bible! What we must do is to investigate the evidences for and against the Bible, for and against Jesus Christ, and weigh the pros and cons. The result will show that the Lord Jesus Christ of the Bible is altogether what He claimed to be and that the Bible is worthy of our entire trust. We must then make the decision, and be willing to make an honest and total commitment to God. The Psalmist is not arrogant when he says, 'You make me wiser than my enemies', or later in verse 99, 'I have more understanding than all my teachers.' What do these two verses really mean? First of all in our verse he is faced with enemies. They are not believers. They reject the Word, the Bible. They say that other books like the Vedas and the Koran are also inspired, so what is so special about your Bible? These are people who reject the Bible outright. You and I therefore as Christians have knowledge of things that others who are not Christians do not have. 'The natural man (or the man without the Spirit) does not receive the things of the Spirit of God, for they are foolishness to him' (1 Corinthians 2:14).

READING THE BIBLE GIVES SPIRITUAL INTELLIGENCE

*verse 99:   I have more understanding **than all** my teachers,
For Your testimonies are my meditation.*

The teachers mentioned in this verse are not the teachers in the biblical sense: '(Christ) gave … some pastors and teachers' (Ephesians 4:11). The Psalmist speaks of ordinary teachers, not spiritual gifts. It is these teachers who, unless they are Christians, are totally void of spiritual intelligence in the Biblical sense of the word. If therefore the writer says that he is wiser than his own teachers, he is speaking of spiritual wisdom, for there is another kind of wisdom. This is what James says, 'This wisdom does not

descend from above, but is earthly, sensual, demonic. …
But the wisdom that is from above is first pure, then
peaceable, gentle, willing to yield, full of mercy and good
fruits, without partiality and without hypocrisy' (James
3:15, 17). Such wisdom from above is not acquired simply by our own intellectual abilities, but is a gift from
heaven.

THIS WISDOM NEVER MAKES PROUD

*verse 100: I understand more **than the ancients**,*
Because I keep Your precepts.

The ancients in this verse are men of long experience. We
must not think that these ancients are the same as our
New Testament elders. An ancient in Israel was simply a
wise old man with long experience. An elder in the New
Testament is a brother in Christ, who has the Holy Spirit
dwelling in him. It is possible of course that even a
present-day older brother is not as spiritually wise as a
younger brother, but the older brother certainly has more
experience. As to wisdom in the sense of spiritual
intelligence coupled with spirituality, this is not always
necessarily connected with age or long experience. To
come back to our verse then. The Psalmist 'had been
taught to observe in heart and life the precepts of the
Lord, and this was more than the most venerable sinner
had ever learned, more than the philosopher of antiquity
had so much as aspired to know. He had the word with
him, and so outstripped his foes; he meditated on it, and
so outran his friends; he practised it, and so outshone his
elders' [13].

IT GUIDES ME IN THE RIGHT WAY

*verse 101: I have restrained my feet **from every** evil way,
That I may keep Your word.*

Here is the practical side of this wisdom – it restrains us from every evil way! In verse 11 we saw that what kept him from sinning was that he hid the Word of God in his heart. It has been said, 'If the Word does not keep you from sin, then sin will keep you from the Word.' We need God's Word every day to guide and direct our steps. The Israelite of old was also deeply impressed with the importance of having that Word before his heart and thoughts all day long. Here is what we read in Deuteronomy 6:6-9, 'These words which I command you today shall be in your heart. You shall teach them diligently to your children, and shall talk of them when you sit in your house, when you walk by the way, when you lie down, and when you rise up. You shall bind them as a sign on your hand. … You shall write them on the doorposts of your house and on your gates.' Good, sound advice for the believer in Christ today!

IT KEEPS ME FROM WANDERING

*verse 102: I have not departed **from Your judgments**,
For You Yourself have taught me.*

Another wonderful result of abiding in the Word, and of the Word abiding in us, is that the Word will preserve us from going astray. 'I have not departed from Your judgments' is the testimony of the writer. The Word of Christ should dwell richly in us (Colossians 3:16), so 'that we should no longer be children, tossed to and fro and carried about with every wind of doctrine, by the trickery of men, in the cunning craftiness of deceitful plotting' (Ephesians 4:14). The secret is that we stay close to the Lord Jesus. He has the words of eternal life. It is so easy to deviate and to be distracted and deceived. 'You Yourself have taught me', continues the verse. We stay close to the Lord so that He may teach us. *'Take time to be holy, speak oft with thy Lord'*, says the old hymn. Do we really take time to be with Him, and to listen to His voice and so be taught what He wants us to do?

THE PROOF OF THE PUDDING IS IN THE EATING

verse 103: **How** *sweet are Your words to my taste,*
Sweeter than honey to my mouth!

Is the writer of these words the same as the one who wrote, 'Oh, taste and see that the LORD is good; blessed is the man who trusts in Him!' (Psalm 34:8)? To experience the sweetness of honey you have to taste it. When our hearts are full of other things, with worldly things, then we have no appetite for the Word. 'A satisfied soul loathes the honeycomb, but to a hungry soul every bitter thing is sweet' (Proverbs 27:7) – it is a good thing when we are hungry enough to accept every bitter thing put before us by our God and Father. Surely this is the result of reading and absorbing the Word of God. It makes us pliable in His hands, docile and willing for His will. For His will is always sweet, good and acceptable and perfect.

IT WILL INFLUENCE MY SENSE OF VALUES

verse 104: **Through Your precepts** *I get understanding;*
Therefore I hate every false way.

'I hate every false way.' This is the result of the daily renewing of our minds by the Holy Spirit. The Spirit uses the Word of God to form our thoughts, to give us a completely new set of values. What we loved before in our unconverted days, we now hate. The Holy Spirit teaches me the true priorities, the true values, and what is really important and of value to the Lord Jesus Christ. However, to hate the false is characteristic of the new life we have received as Christians, but that is not the sum total. There is also the positive side: to delight in that which is good. Paul says, 'For I delight in the law of God according to the inward man' (Romans 7:22). The ultimate secret is, of course, that it is not even sufficient to delight in the law of God, but to be able to do it. Paul found that, as a regenerate believer in the Gospel, he had sin dwelling in him. He struggled hard to make his 'flesh' do the will of God, but failed. He so much wanted to please the Lord, but he found he had no strength of his own. But then he discovered the secret – not in his own strength, but 'through Jesus Christ our Lord.' And so Paul capitulated and surrendered himself totally to the Lord.

ב

14. NUN – verses 105-112

Meaning: Fish

Derivation: The name of this letter in Syriac, Aramaic and Arabic, denotes a fish, which appears to have been intended by its original form. In the Phoenician alphabet its common form is this.

Numerical value: Fifty (50)

Significance: Some have seen the idea of continuity in this letter and its meaning; others see in it the meaning of 'strength and energy of the fish being able to go against the current'.

God's Word gives direction

IT IS LIKE A LAMP

*verse 105: Your word is **a lamp** to my feet*
And a light to my path.

The idea of giving direction is seen at once in this well-known verse. We all realise that we need help and direction in our Christian life and walk day by day. How do we get this help and direction? Only through the Word of God. For our Bible study we always need spiritual illumination, light given by the Holy Spirit so that we may see things as He sees them. The only light in the Holy

Place of the Tabernacle was the light shed by the lamp-stand, which is a beautiful type of the activity of the Holy Spirit. Israel in the wilderness was guided by a cloud during the day, and by a pillar of fire during the night. This again is a beautiful symbol of the Holy Spirit's activity. We could say that a lamp is needed during the night-time, and the light of the sun during the day. We need both! The path is the course we take when our feet actually execute our brain's directions. In every sense we are dependent upon His help to direct our feet in His path, and then daily, during times of prosperity (day) and times of adversity (night), we need the light that His Holy Spirit gives us.

It helps me make decisions

verse 106: **I have sworn** *and confirmed*
                That I will keep Your righteous judgments.

'I have sworn and confirmed'; this sounds very much like making a vow. The Psalmist is also very sure of himself, 'I will keep'. There is only one Man who could ever have rightly pronounced such words, and that is the Lord Jesus Christ. 'Behold, I have come-—in the volume of the book it is written of Me—to do Your will, O God' (Hebrews 10:7). And then, 'I have finished the work which You have given Me to do' (John 17:4). I do not believe that it is right for a New Testament believer to make a vow. Only if we have not really understood the plague of our own hearts, would we dare trust ourselves to be able ever to perform what we have promised. It is better to tell the Lord that we love Him truly, and want to please Him, but that we need Him to help us. 'For I have the desire to do what is good, but I cannot carry it out' (Romans 7:18, NIV). 'For it is God who works in you both to will and to do for His good pleasure' (Philippians 2:13).

IT HELPS ME ENDURE

verse 107: **I am afflicted** *very much;*
Revive me, O LORD, according to Your word.

The word 'afflicted' (*anah*) here is the same as in verse 67 (see the verse); it can also mean 'depressed'. The writer feels very much afflicted. Does he think he is afflicted beyond his ability to endure? Just because we are Christians does not mean that we will be spared the afflictions and sicknesses and troubles like others. But God understands and gives us grace to bear and to endure. The Psalmist prays, 'Give me life by Your word.' He does not know about that abundant life that Jesus Christ came to bring and to manifest, for that life is the life of Jesus Christ Himself. The New Testament believer is indwelt by the Lord Jesus, which is why we can say, 'Christ is my life' (see Galatians 2:20). 'In this you greatly rejoice, though now for a little while, if need be, you have been grieved by various trials, that the genuineness of your faith, being much more precious than gold that perishes, though it is tested by fire, may be found to praise, honour, and glory at the revelation of Jesus Christ' (1 Peter 1:6-7).

IT HELPS ME OFFER PRAISE

verse 108: Accept, I pray, **the freewill offerings** *of my*
mouth, O LORD,
And teach me Your judgments.

'Whoever offers praise glorifies Me; and to him who orders his conduct aright I will show the salvation of God' (Psalm 50:23). A Christian is the only human being who can really *sing* and be heard in heaven. It is the redeemed who have every reason to sing. Even in the Old Testament we read of saints offering praise to Jehovah. How much more should we, New Testament believers, obey the encouragement in Hebrews 13:15, 'Therefore by Him let us continually offer the sacrifice of praise to God, that is, the fruit of our lips, giving thanks to His name.' When should a believer sing? On every possible occasion. Paul and Silas were able to sing praises even while suffering physical pain: 'At midnight Paul and Silas were praying and singing hymns to God, and the prisoners were listening to them' (Acts 16:25). Where should Christians sing praises? Wherever they find themselves. Why should believers sing praises? Because it glorifies God, and it is a testimony to others. Praises from the lips of redeemed persons are simply the fruit of the Holy Spirit's activity. Can He use your lips? And in meetings too when the Assembly gathers together?

IT HELPS ME FACE LIFE EVERY DAY

verse 109: **My life** *is continually in my hand,*
Yet I do not forget Your law.

The Hebrew word *nephesh* can be translated soul, breath, body, creature, or simply life. The Hebrew text here has, 'My life is in my palm continually.' The life here encompasses everything I am and do each day. My total being – me! The believer is always practically in the very jaws of death! We have countless spiritual enemies in the powers of darkness. The verse is a Hebraism signifying a condition of extreme danger. Paul knew that 'in every city … chains and tribulations await me' (Acts 20:23). His attitude was expressed as follows, 'None of these things move me, I am ready not only to be bound, but also to die at Jerusalem for the name of the Lord Jesus' (see Acts 21:13). It has been said of Paul, 'He could look "tribulation, or persecution, or peril, or sword" in the face; and, while he *"carried his soul continually in his hand"*, in true Christian heroism, in the most exalted triumph of faith, he could say in the name of himself and his companions in tribulation, "Nay, in all these things we are more than conquerors"' [3]. Paul also said, 'I die daily' (1 Corinthians 15:31). But like the Psalmist, so also Paul could say, 'O LORD, ... teach me Your judgments' (verse 108) '... yet I do not forget Your law' (verse 109). He wanted to know what the Lord wanted him to do in every situation.

IT HELPS ME CONQUER EVIL AND SIN

*verse 110: The wicked **have laid** a snare for me,*
Yet I have not strayed from Your precepts.

The theme of being surrounded by enemies continues in this verse. They are scheming and plotting and planning to make the believer stumble and fall. How much indeed we therefore need the Word of God to direct us day by day and moment by moment. The apostle Peter says, 'Be sober, be vigilant; because your adversary the devil walks about like a roaring lion, seeking whom he may devour. Resist him, steadfast in the faith, knowing that the same sufferings are experienced by your brotherhood in the world' (1 Peter 5:8-9). How then can we resist and overcome the enemy? Only by using the Word of God as the sword of the Spirit, and like our Lord Jesus Christ being able to say, 'It is written.' If we do that, then we can join the Psalmist and give this testimony, '... yet I have not strayed from Your precepts.' The Lord will keep us, as we stay close to Him.

IT WILL ENRICH ME SPIRITUALLY

*verse 111: Your testimonies **I have taken as a heritage***
forever,
For they are the rejoicing of my heart.

The enemy seeks to rob us of any spiritual blessing or possession we may have. We have received an immense inheritance in and with the Lord Jesus Christ. The enemy cannot take away our salvation and eternal life which we have in Christ, but we can lose our crown and our reward. 'Blessed be the God and Father of our Lord Jesus Christ, who according to His abundant mercy has begotten us again to a living hope through the resurrection of Jesus Christ from the dead, to an inheritance incorruptible and undefiled and that does not fade away, reserved in heaven for you, who are kept by the power of God ...' (1 Peter 1:3-5). This is our inheritance as New Testament believers and it is heavenly, whereas the believers of the Old Testament looked forward to an earthly inheritance. How infinitely more blessed we are therefore! We can echo the words of the Psalmist, '... for they are the rejoicing of my heart.' Peter continues in that first chapter, verse 6, 'In this you greatly rejoice (i.e. in that inheritance), though now for a little while, if need be, you have been grieved by various trials.'

IT HELPS ME DO GOD'S WILL

verse 112: ***I have inclined*** *my heart to perform Your*
            statutes
            Forever, to the very end.

We are back at verse 106 where he makes this solemn vow, 'I have sworn and confirmed.' But in this verse 112 it seems there is a noticeable advance. He is not so confident in himself, for he has learned to bow his heart before the Lord. There is no self-will or self-confidence any more. His heart and his entire being are in the hands of the Lord. As long as he remains in those hands he will be able to do the Lord's statutes. Remember, a statute is a divine direction to obtain man's obedience! The Lord is faithful until the end.

ס

15. SAMECH - verses 113-120

Meaning: Support

Derivation: The name of this letter denotes a prop, or a support, to which this letter answers in shape in the Phoenician alphabet.

Numerical value: Sixty (60)

Significance: We remember that the Ephraimites pronounced the word *shibboleth* (whose first letter *shin* sounds like a 'sh') as though it began with this letter *samech*, sounding like an 's', and were consequently put to death (Judges 12:6). From this incident we learn that we should not insist that everybody should be obliged to pronounce our 'shibboleth' the way we do!

God's Word for our support

IT GIVES SPIRITUAL DISCERNMENT

*verse 113: I hate **the double-minded**,*
    But I love Your law.

Notice the contrasts in this verse – hate and love! These are very decisive expressions. He certainly has deep convictions! The writer to the Epistle to the Hebrews was longing for his readers to grow in spiritual discernment. He said, 'But solid food belongs to those who are of full age, that is, those who by reason of use have their senses exercised to discern both good and evil' (Hebrews 5:14). Instead of 'vain thoughts' (AV) the Hebrew word is translated as double-minded, i.e. a divided heart. Actually, the French Bible has 'doubles de coeur' – double hearted. James gives us this warning about a divided heart, '... he who doubts is like a wave of the sea driven and tossed by the wind. For let not that man suppose that he will receive anything from the Lord; he is a double-minded man, unstable in all his ways' (James 1:6-8). This kind of attitude is hateful to the Psalmist. Is it also hateful to you, my dear reader?

It acts like a shield of faith
*verse 114: You are **my hiding place** and my shield;*
I hope in Your word.

Here we have the defensive attitude expressed in the words 'You are my hiding place.' There are times when we should flee from the evil one and temptation; but we need our shield of faith when we are on the offensive. The Lord is both to us: hiding place and shield. The Lord protects us during the day from the sun, and during the night from the moon (Psalm 121:6). 'When the enemy comes in like a flood, The Spirit of the LORD will lift up a standard against him' (Isaiah 59:19). These verses certainly show that those who 'hope in Your word' do not hope in vain!

It helps me stand and resist

*verse 115: **Depart** from me, you evildoers,*
For I will keep the commandments of my God!

So, having put on the complete armour of God, the sword of the Spirit and the shield of faith, we must now stand against the artifices of the devil. 'Depart from me, you evildoers', says the writer. We are able to say the same in the name of the Lord Jesus. 'Resist the devil and he will flee from you' (James 4:7), is the promise we can claim. It is not enough just to hate double-mindedness but we must also hate evil in any form. In this verse we find the only mention in this long Psalm of this intimate expression 'my God'. He has this intimate fellowship with the Lord and wants to do His will, and keep His commandments. It is only in the measure that we give ourselves to do His will, that we shall be able also to resist evil and evildoers.

IT HELPS ME TO REMAIN STANDING

verse 116: **Uphold me** *according to Your word, that I may live;*
And do not let me be ashamed of my hope.

Verses 116 and 117 carry the theme of this section of eight verses: 'uphold me', 'hold me up'. The Word of God gives us the support we need day by day to live the Christian life. 'Fear not, for I am with you; be not dismayed, for I am your God. I will strengthen you, yes, I will help you, I will uphold you with My righteous right hand' (Isaiah 41:10). What a wonderful promise for us to lay hold of! He who gives life, also sustains it. We are 'kept by the power of God' (1 Peter 1:5). Indeed, all our springs are in Him (Psalm 87:7). 'Our sufficiency is from God' (2 Corinthians 3:5). If we trust in His precious Word we will never be put to shame.

IT WILL SAVE

verse 117: **Hold me up**, *and I shall be safe,*
And I shall observe Your statutes continually.

I remember in my childhood standing on the ice of a canal that was frozen over. How slippery it was and how difficult it was to stay upright without falling. How good it felt when my father was there beside me holding me up, helping me take my first strides on my skates! The strong hand of my father was there to support me. There is first of all the sense of weakness we may feel, and then the realisation that there are slippery paths before us, full of dangers and pitfalls. Our safety depends every moment upon the upholding power of our Lord and Saviour. 'The eternal God is your refuge, and underneath are the everlasting arms; He will thrust out the enemy from before you' (Deuteronomy 33:27).

IT GIVES ME VICTORY THROUGH JESUS CHRIST

verse 118: **You reject** *all those who stray from Your statutes, For their deceit is falsehood.*

Is this a prophetic view of the future victory of the Lord Jesus Christ when all His enemies will be made His footstool (Psalm 110:1)? The Cross of Calvary is the greatest display of Christ's victory over the powers of darkness. For the time being this victory has not yet been universally manifested because God is merciful even to enemies, even to those who 'stray from His statutes'. He wants them to repent and therefore 'delays' that final day of judgment. However, mark the character of those mentioned in this verse – 'they stray from God's statutes'. Not in their minds as it were through ignorance, but in their hearts and through obstinacy. They deliberately sray from God. They are like those who once said, 'We will not have this Man to reign over us' (Luke 19:14). They say, 'We do not desire the knowledge of Your ways' (Job 21:14). They are justly called in verse 119 'the wicked'! 'Their deceit is falsehood' is another way of saying, '… evil men and impostors will grow worse and worse, deceiving and being deceived' (2 Timothy 3:13).

IT SHOWS ME WHAT SIN REALLY IS

*verse 119: You put away all the wicked of the earth **like***
dross;
  Therefore I love Your testimonies.

Today there are those in the Christian profession 'having a form of godliness but denying its power' (2 Timothy 3:5). Paul adds, 'From such people turn away!' It is said of Israel, 'Son of man, the house of Israel has become dross to Me; … Therefore thus says the Lord GOD: "Because you have all become dross, … I will gather you in My anger and in My fury, and I will leave you there and melt you"' (Ezekiel 22:18-20). We are living in the last days, possibly the 'last hour' before Jesus comes to take His Bride home. These are days of apostasy and departure from the faith. We must therefore 'test the spirits, whether they are of God' (1 John 4:1). We shall be able to discern these false spirits only when we know what the Word says. 'Therefore I love Your testimonies' is the positive attitude taken by the Psalmist. We do well to follow his example!

IT WILL KEEP ME FROM SIN

*verse 120: My flesh **trembles** for fear of You,*
  And I am afraid of Your judgments.

What do you think of this? Is our loving heavenly Father to be feared? We think that, as Father, He will overlook sin; He will not punish sin in believers. He punishes the wicked, yes. But believers who are His own dear children? It is a totally false supposition that our God and our Father does not have to be feared. Meditate on the following verses, 'Therefore, having these promises, beloved, let us cleanse ourselves from all filthiness of the flesh and spirit, perfecting holiness in the fear of God' (2 Corinthians 7:1). '… work out your own salvation with fear and trembling; for it is God who works in you both to will and to do for His good pleasure' (Philippians 2:12-13). 'And if you call on the Father, who without partiality judges according to each one's work, conduct yourselves throughout the time of your stay here in fear' (1 Peter 1:17). 'There is no fear in love; but perfect love casts out fear' (1 John 4:18). The above verses prove that believers should have a healthy fear of the Father, just as a child who loves his father also fears the just punishment he deserves when he acts in disobedience to his father's will. We also fear to grieve and sadden someone we love very much. 'I am afraid of Your judgments', says the Psalmist. With the help and the support the Lord gives us through His precious Word, we can experience victory over our spiritual enemies, avoid pitfalls and dangers, avoid being deceived by false teaching, and be kept sensitive to His will and Word to obey it in our daily lives.

Division Six

VERSES 121-144
IN THE SCHOOL OF THE SPIRIT OF GOD

16. *Ayin*   verses 121-128

      God's Word is a well of refreshment.

17. *Peh*   verses 129-136

      God's Word gives power for testimony.

18. *Tsaddi*   verses 137-144

      God's Word brings us near to Him.

16. AYIN – verses 121-128

Meaning: Well, Eye or Vision

Derivation: The ancient form of the letter resembled an eye. The word *ayin* means eye and, by extension, vision (in the sense of sight). But as in English we might speak of "tears welling up in his eyes", so in Hebrew the word is also used to refer to a well, spring or fountain.

Numerical value: Seventy (70)

Significance: 'Rivers of water run down from my eyes (*ayin*)', says the Psalmist in verse 136 of our Psalm, so profuse were his tears. Whilst these tears flowed in sorrow, when Abraham's servant said, 'Behold, here I stand by the well (*ayin*) of water' (Genesis 24:13), the plentiful supply brought refreshment to a whole city.

God's Word is a well of refreshment

The first section in this division of the Psalm, 'in the School of the Spirit of God', introduces us to the divine Teacher.

128

PRINCIPLES FIRST, THEN PRACTICE

verse 121: ***I have done*** *justice and righteousness;*
Do not leave me to my oppressors.

We must have an unaccusing conscience in order to be able to echo what the Psalmist claims for himself, 'I have done justice and righteousness.' It is not enough to know that we have been justified by faith, now we must live just lives. Principles are to be translated into practice. John says, 'For if our heart condemns us, God is greater than our heart, and knows all things. Beloved, if our heart does not condemn us, we have confidence toward God' (1 John 3:20-21). What verse 20 says is in fact this: that if I am conscious that I have failed putting into practice what true love really is toward my brother or sister (see verses 17-18), how much more does God know my failure! Unless I confess and rectify this situation, I cannot count on His answering my prayers (verses 21-22). The Psalmist is confident that the Lord will not leave him to his oppressors. We too can have this confidence in the Lord's tender care day by day.

IN CHRIST I AM SECURE

verse 122: ***Be surety*** *for Your servant for good;*
Do not let the proud oppress me.

This is a true expression of confidence! He prays that the Lord might be his surety. We know that the Lord is our surety! Although we may be very conscious of our many failures and short-comings, we also know that *He* has settled all our debts and borne all our weaknesses in His body on the cross. In the words of the apostle Paul, we hear Christ say to the Father, 'If he has wronged you or owes anything, put that on my account' (Philemon 18). We will always remain debtors to His love. Jesus takes our place in the presence of our God and Father when Satan comes to accuse us. The Lord Jesus is there our 'surety' and our precious 'advocate', and no accusation against us will stand. 'Do not let the proud oppress me', no doubt this refers also to our accuser, the adversary, the devil. We can be confident that no one can 'bring a charge against God's elect', for 'It is God who justifies' (Romans 8:33).

THERE IS NEED FOR PATIENCE AND SUBMISSION

verse 123: **My eyes** *fail from seeking Your salvation*
And Your righteous word.

Here we have the true meaning of the 16th letter, *ayin*! In both Hebrew and Arabic it means eye. The writer says that his eyes fail. Sometimes when you have looked at an object for a long time, your eyes fail and become tired and dim. The Psalmist had been weeping, and waiting, and watching for the help of the Lord to come to his rescue. His faith was tried. How wonderful to know that if our eyes fail, the Lord never fails, nor do His eyes fail! Trials and testing teach us patience, and give us experience. When we feel we have waited too long, let us remember the Lord Jesus in Psalm 69:3, 'I am weary with my crying; my throat is dry; my eyes fail while I wait for my God.' 'For consider Him who endured such hostility from sinners against Himself, lest you become weary and discouraged in your souls' (Hebrews 12:3). Take courage then, dear brother, dear sister: 'For you have need of endurance, so that after you have done the will of God, you may receive the promise' (Hebrews 10:36).

THERE IS NEED FOR COMPASSION

verse 124: **Deal** *with Your servant according to Your mercy,*
And teach me Your statutes.

The writer is conscious of his weakness, slowness to grasp the Lord's instructions, and pleads for 'mercy'. The French version calls this 'goodness' or 'kindness'. No doubt we are all conscious of our need for His kindness and patience with us. Psalm 103 is wonderfully encouraging here: 'The LORD is merciful and gracious, slow to anger, and abounding in mercy. ... As a father pities his children, so the LORD pities those who fear Him. For He knows our frame; He remembers that we are dust' (verses 8, 13-14). Our place before Him is that of a servant. This is indeed our privilege. How gracious of the Lord to call us His friends: 'No longer do I call you servants, for a servant does not know what his master is doing; but I have called you friends, for all things that I heard from My Father I have made known to you' (John 15:15). '... and teach me Your statutes' continues our verse. How wonderful to know that He will daily teach us the lessons we need, so that we may grow in our spiritual lives.

THERE IS NEED FOR INSTRUCTION

*verse 125: I **am Your servant**;*
Give me understanding,
That I may know Your testimonies.

Continuing in his place as a servant he asks for understanding of His testimonies. That is, he wants to grow in his understanding of what the Lord is and what he ought to be day by day. We all need that daily spiritual intelligence in order to discern the will of the Lord. But in order to know His will we must be willing to accept the conditions: 'I beseech you therefore, brethren, by the mercies of God, that you present your bodies a living sacrifice, holy, acceptable to God, which is your reasonable service. And do not be conformed to this world, but be transformed by the renewing of your mind, that you may prove what is that good and acceptable and perfect will of God' (Romans 12:1-2). Three times now we have seen the repetition of the word 'servant' in this 16th section: verses 122, 124 and 125. It is the position an inferior takes. It is also the position a pupil takes in relation to his teacher. We do well to remember that we shall remain 'pupils needing to learn' all our lives. Unless we are taught ourselves we shall never be able to teach others.

THE NEED FOR COMMUNION BETWEEN MASTER AND SERVANT

verse 126: **It is time** *for You to act, O LORD,*
For they have regarded Your law as void.

God as LORD is here addressed. One of the first things we must learn as pupils in the school of the Spirit of God is to recognise and submit to the Lordship of Jesus Christ. We may read of the Lord Jesus' wonderful condescension in calling us His friends, but He is still Lord. In John 13:13 we read, 'You call me Teacher and Lord, and you say well, for so I am.' Here then we see clearly that on the one hand He invites us to a wonderful and precious intimacy with Him, as One with His friends, but this intimacy should never degenerate into a kind of mere familiarity with Him. If He calls us His brothers, we do not therefore call Him our 'Brother'!! Today we see this idea of levelling out and of equalising. Jesus is reduced to a mere superman. He is addressed in the same way that we address a beggar, and an inferior. There is very little respect and reverence with regard to His Person. Let us by all means enjoy this precious communion with Him, but ever remember Who He is.

NEVER COMPROMISE

verse 127: **Therefore** *I love Your commandments*
More than gold, yes, than fine gold!

Here we have a resolution based upon an observation. The pupil is learning fast! He has found that in total submission to his divine Teacher he is growing more and more in understanding of divine things.

Have I an object, Lord, below,
   Which would divide my heart from Thee;
Which would divert its even flow
In answer to Thy constancy?
   Oh, teach me quickly to return,
   And cause my heart afresh to burn!

(George West Frazer, 1830-1896)

We are in fact repeating in modern language what the Psalmist is saying, 'I love Your commandments more than gold, yes, than fine gold!' We cannot compromise the precious Word for gold, even for fine gold, or whatever could be compared to something precious which would usurp that Word in our affections. We have made the discovery that His Word is more precious than anything else, that is why we love it. Notice the Psalmist does not say that he is always faithful in keeping it, but that he loves it. That is where we also must commence!

HE DOES ALL THINGS WELL

verse 128: **Therefore** *all Your precepts concerning all things*
   I consider to be right;
   I hate every false way.

Again the sentence begins with the same word in the Hebrew which we have rendered in English as therefore or so. It still speaks of a conclusion. The Psalmist is very intense in his expressions here. Notice the word all is repeated three times: 'all Your precepts', 'all things', 'every false way'. It is a very good thing to be absolutely convinced about what the Bible teaches. Paul writes to Timothy, 'But you must continue in the things which you have learned and been assured of, knowing from whom you have learned them' (2 Timothy 3:14). The apostle Paul was assured about many things. For instance in Romans 8:28 he writes, 'And we know that all things work together for good to those who love God, to those who are the called according to His purpose.' Further in verse 38 he says, 'For I am persuaded...' Do you have strong convictions? Are they based on the Scriptures? Now we can see both the reason and the necessity for Bible-study, that we might be established in the Word. Let us then submit to our divine Teacher, the blessed Holy Spirit.

17. PEH – verses 129-136

Meaning: Mouth

Derivation: The name of this letter probably signifies a mouth.

Numerical value: Eighty (80)

Significance: Our mouths are used to testify for and of the Lord, as true believers. Our Christian witness is rendered both by our lips and by our lives.

God's Word gives power for testimony

The second section in this division of the Psalm introduces us to our divine textbook.

THE MORE I LEARN, THE LESS I SEEM TO KNOW

verse 129: Your testimonies **are wonderful;**
              Therefore my soul keeps them.

The Bible is a marvel and a miracle. Sixty-six books, written by more than forty writers over a period of 1500 years, in Hebrew, Aramaic and Greek, yet one spirit permeates the whole – the Holy Spirit Who inspired the theme. The Gideons International publishers [1] have the following in

---

[1] The Gideons International within the British Isles, Western House, George Street, Lutterworth LE17 4EE

135

the front of their Bibles, 'The Bible reveals the mind of God, the state of man, the way of salvation, the doom of the ungodly, and the happiness of believers. Its teaching is holy, its precepts are binding, its histories are true, its prophecies are certain and its decisions immutable. Read it to be wise, believe it to be safe and practise it to be holy. It contains light to direct you, armour to protect you, food to sustain you and comfort to cheer you. It is the traveller's map, the pilgrim's stay, the pilot's compass, the builder's plan, the soldier's sword, the shepherd's staff, the sailor's anchor and the Christian's charter. It should fill the memory, rule the heart and guide the feet. Here, Paradise is restored, Heaven is opened, and the gates of hell disclosed. Christ is its grand Subject, our good its design, redemption its plan and the glory of God its end. It is given to you here in this life, it will be opened in the judgment, and is established for ever. It involves the highest responsibility, will reward the greatest labour and condemns all who trifle with its sacred contents. Come to it with awe, a storehouse of food, a paradise of glory, a rose of rare fragrance, a river of joy, a life-giving fountain, a wheel with sixty-six spokes (books) each leading to Christ, its centre and hub. These sixty-six books form a splendid library, all in one cover, which can be carried in the pocket. It is the masterpiece of all literature; it is published in more languages, and is loved and read by more people, than any other book.' Seeing that I could not write anything better, I am glad to quote the above. The more we read it, the more we want to read it. The more we understand it, the more we realise our ignorance and need for more knowledge. It is an inexhaustible Textbook. Yes, indeed we can echo the words of the Psalmist, 'Your testimonies are wonderful.'

THE BLIGHT OF SPIRITUAL INTELLECTUALISM

verse 130: **The entrance** *of Your words gives light*
It gives understanding to the simple.

The word translated 'entrance' may also be rendered opening, open and transparent statement, declaration, sometimes even illustration. The Bible has limitless applications to limitless circumstances. All the spiritual light known in this dark world has come from the Word. News from mission-fields show that this Word, preached to unintelligent and uncultivated minds, often gives an enlargement and elevation of thought, which is the earnest of the restoration of man to his original glory. It is not only the would-be intellectual, or the Bible-critic and those skilled in Higher Criticism, who have understanding, because some of them might be completely void of spiritual life. It gives understanding to the simple! This does not mean to the idiot, or the simple-minded, but those who in their own eyes realise their lack of understanding and their utter dependence upon the illumination of the Holy Spirit. Let us listen to what the apostle Paul has to say in 1 Corinthians 3:18-19, 'Let no one deceive himself. If anyone among you seems to be wise in this age, let him become a fool that he may become wise. For the wisdom of this world is foolishness with God.'

WE OPEN OUR MOUTHS AND HE WILL FILL THEM

verse 131: I opened **my mouth** *and panted,*
For I longed for Your commandments.

Here then we have the true meaning of the 17th letter of the alphabet. We open our mouths either to speak or to eat or drink. The Psalmist says that he 'panted with his mouth'. What does panting mean? The dictionary says, among others, that it is 'to yearn for, or after a thing.'

Here is a believer who just longs for the Word of God. Do we have that kind of hunger and thirst after the living Word when we awaken in the morning? Psalm 87:7 reads, 'All my springs are in You.' Nothing else and nothing less can satisfy our spiritual hunger and thirst other than the precious word of God. 'As the deer pants for the water brooks, so pants my soul for You, O God. ... My soul thirsts for You; my flesh longs for You in a dry and thirsty land where there is no water. ... I spread out my hands to You; my soul longs for You like a thirsty land' (Psalm 42:1; 63:1; 143:6).

Always pray before reading and studying

verse 132: **Look upon** *me and be merciful to me,*
    As Your custom is toward those who love Your
    name.

You will remember from my Introduction that we find no mention of any of the synonyms of the Word in verses 90, 122 and 132! The Psalmist has been concentrating on the preciousness of the Word and his need for studying it in order to understand it and so be able to render his testimony. Here he is on his knees! How necessary indeed it is to pray. Bible study should always be accompanied by prayer, otherwise we risk becoming too theoretical. Yes, we all need His favour and mercy day by day. Sometimes we do not feel like reading the Bible or studying it. Often, whilst reading, our thoughts wander and we take nothing in. Often we have forgotten next day what we have read the previous day! His mercy is especially for those who are conscious of all this weakness. However, think of a colander we may use in our kitchens. If there is some dirt in it, the water will no doubt pass through it and nothing of the water remain in it, but the colander is cleaner! The same applies to us; we may feel that we have profited nothing from reading the Bible one day, but never forget that the water of the Word has passed through us and we are definitely the cleaner for it!

THE FIRST LESSON: PRACTICAL HOLINESS

*verse 133: Direct **my steps** by Your word,*
And let no iniquity have dominion over me.

It is true to say that if the Word dominates me and my actions, then sin cannot dominate me. The apostle Paul tells us in Romans 6:12, 'Therefore do not let sin reign in your mortal body, that you should obey it in its lusts.' Practical holiness can only be experienced as we obey the Word of God, and submit to the Holy Spirit's instructions. 'The steps of a man are established by Jehovah, and he delighteth in his way: though he fall, he shall not be utterly cast down, for Jehovah upholdeth his hand' (Psalm 37:23-24, N.Tr.). One of the first lessons we learn in the Christian life is indeed that the Lord our God is holy, and therefore He wants us to be holy in our behaviour. 'Be holy, for I am holy' (1 Peter 1:16). It is our responsibility to pray constantly the prayer in our verse, 'Direct my steps by Your word.' And the verse in Psalm 37 is the answer from the Lord, 'The steps of a man are established by Jehovah.'

THE SECOND LESSON: DELIVERANCE FROM SIN IN ANY FORM

*verse 134: **Redeem me** from the oppression of man,*
That I may keep Your precepts.

Deliverance is here sought from what worldly and ungodly men and women can do to us. We all need deliverance from the fear of man, from the opinions of men, from the fashion of this world, from worldliness. The Hebrew verb can also be translated 'cut me loose', or 'ransom me'. This is helpful, for we can so easily become the slaves of men, and the way the world does things. We perhaps like to be popular with our unbelieving friends. But the Christian dare not compromise. We do not want to be obnoxious with superior airs, yet neither do we want to lose our testimony by pleasing the world. The Lord Jesus Christ Himself warns us that He 'did not come to bring peace but a sword', with regard to our family relations. He says 'a man's enemies will be those of his own household' (Matthew 10:34-36). If therefore, in the words of this verse, 'we may keep His precepts', we must decide: Whom shall we please? The Lord Jesus, or the world, or ourselves? Deliver us, dear Lord, from any wrong thing that would dominate us.

THE THIRD LESSON: OUR PERFECT ACCEPTANCE BEFORE GOD

*verse 135: Make **Your face** shine upon Your servant,
And teach me Your statutes.*

How blessed to know that 'we have access by faith into' His 'grace in which we stand' (Romans 5:2). Yes, indeed, we are 'accepted in the Beloved' (Ephesians 1:6). A friend tells the following story: 'One morning on the farm, I saw the strangest looking lamb – it had six legs! and the last two were hanging helplessly as though paralysed. But when the farmer caught the lamb the mystery was explained. The lamb did not originally belong to the ewe that now cared for it. The ewe had had a lamb which was bitten by a snake and died. This lamb that I saw was an orphan and needed a mother's care. But at first the bereft ewe refused to have anything to do with it. She sniffed at it when it was brought to her, then pushed it away, as if saying, "That is not our family odour." The farmer skinned the lamb that had died and very carefully drew the fleece over the living lamb. This left the hind-leg coverings dragging loose. Thus covered, the lamb was brought again to the ewe. She smelled it once more and this time seemed thoroughly satisfied and adopted it as her own.' It seems to me to be a beautiful picture of the grace of God. We are all outcasts and have no claim upon His love. But God's Son, the 'Lamb of God', has died for us and now we who believe are dressed up in the fleece of the Lamb Who died. Thus God has accepted us in Him. This whole idea is beautifully expressed in the following,

So dear, so very dear to God,
More dear I cannot be;
The love wherewith He loves His Son,
Such is His love to me.

So near, so very near to God,
Nearer I could not be,
For in the person of His Son,
I am as near as He.

(Captain Catesby Paget, 1809-1878)

THE FOURTH LESSON: COMPASSION FOR LOST SOULS

verse 136: **Rivers** *of water run down from my eyes,*
Because men do not keep Your law.

What a precious verse we have here in the Old Testament! It is an amazing expression of the compassionate heart of the Psalmist for those who 'do not keep Your law'. He is so deeply moved for them that he says, 'Rivers of waters run down from my eyes' for them! The NIV is far too general when it says, 'Streams of tears flow from my eyes, for your law is not obeyed.' It leaves out completely the Psalmist's sorrow at people's active disobedience represented by the pronoun 'men' ('people' or 'they' in other translations), which the Hebrew shows in the word *lō-shameru*, 'men do not keep'. When the Lord Jesus came near Jerusalem, we read in Luke 19:41 that, when He saw the city, He wept over it.

On three occasions we see that Jesus wept:

a. John 11:35 – He wept over a household;
b. Luke 19:41 – He wept over a city;
c. Hebrews 5:7 – He wept being in a lost world.

From this we see that the Lord Jesus is never indifferent to human needs and problems. Do you have this compassion for the lost, dear reader? Have you ever wept over a lost soul? Have you ever said to the Lord, 'Here am I, Lord, send me'? This whole section 17 speaks of God giving us power in order to testify. Verses 133-136 have shown us what is needed for those who would seek to speak to others of Christ: they must live holy lives, and know personally the power of the Holy Spirit in daily deliverance from the slavery of sin, and have the deep assurance of being totally accepted in the worthiness of Christ before God, and have the same compassion that filled their Master. Do we qualify?

צ

18. TSADDI – verses 137-144

Meaning: Side or Assistance

Derivation: This letter is thought by some to resemble a fish hook. Its name is very similar to the word *tsad*, meaning 'side' (Deuteronomy 31:26), 'beside' (Joshua 12:9; Ruth 2:14) or sometimes an 'adversary' (Numbers 33:55; Judges 2:3). In the Arabic *sadd*, very similar to Hebrew, means 'to turn oneself from anyone', or 'to turn to him the side, not the face', hence 'to oppose oneself to anyone'.

Numerical value: Ninety (90)

Significance: Perhaps its shape would remind us of Jesus' call to His disciples to become 'fishers of men' (Matthew 4:19) – drawing people to Christ. The meaning of the word reminds us that the One to Whose side we are drawn remains beside us for our assistance at all times.

God's Word brings us near to Him

The final section in this division of the Psalm introduces us to the topics for study in the school of the Spirit of God.

THE JUSTICE OF GOD

verse 137: **Righteous** *are You, O LORD,*
And upright are Your judgments.

How wonderful to realise that God's righteousness through Jesus Christ has set me in a place of nearness to Himself! Righteousness is one of God's attributes. He must punish sin, otherwise He cannot rule over a moral universe and His holiness would be outraged. In Romans 4:5 we read, 'But to him who does not work but believes on Him who justifies the ungodly, his faith is accounted for righteousness.' As the holiness and righteousness of God's character demand the death of the sinner, our Lord Jesus Christ took our place and was 'made … sin for us, that we might become the righteousness of God in Him' (2 Corinthians 5:21). 'Mercy and truth have met together; righteousness and peace have kissed' (Psalm 85:10). Once more we are taught our complete acceptance before or in Christ, as we saw earlier in verse 135.

THE FAITHFULNESS OF GOD

verse 138: Your testimonies, **which You have**
commanded,
Are righteous and very faithful.

God's faithfulness is:

a. based upon a faithful covenant;
b. confirmed by faithful promises;
c. executed by a faithful redeemer.

From that moment before the foundation of the world, when He set His love upon you and me and chose us in Christ, His love has never changed, and never will change! We are so often fickle and changeable, but God loves us just as much now as He did when we first came to know the Lord Jesus as our own personal Saviour and Lord. My dear fellow-Christian, let us encourage one another with these words, 'If we are faithless, He remains faithful; He cannot deny Himself' (2 Timothy 2:13).

ZEAL FOR THE HONOUR OF HIS NAME

*verse 139: My zeal **has consumed me**,*
Because my enemies have forgotten Your words.

David, as a prophet, spoke similar words as coming from the mouth of the Lord Jesus Christ, in Psalm 69:9, 'Because zeal for Your house has eaten me up, and the reproaches of those who reproach You have fallen on me.' We were all indeed by nature enemies and thus brought reproach upon the holy character of God. But the Lord Jesus has borne that reproach – that shame – that sin – in His very own body on the cross of Calvary and paid the penalty that we deserved. Blessed Saviour and Redeemer! How can we now show our gratitude to Him? Surely, by being zealous for the honour of His name, by proclaiming His wonderful virtues and character as Saviour to lost sinners! Are we indeed 'fervent in spirit, serving the Lord' (Romans 12:11)? We are often put to shame by false, but zealous, workers of the devil's lies. Think of the Communists, the Mormons and the Jehovah's Witnesses and their zeal. Paul said a similar thing of the Jews who opposed the Gospel of God's Grace, 'For I bear them witness that they have a zeal for God, but not according to knowledge' (Romans 10:2). There is a negative and a positive zeal, and Paul explains this in Galatians 4:17-18, 'They zealously court you, but for no good; … But it is good to be zealous in a good thing always.' My dear friend, are you zealous in winning souls for Christ?

THE PURITY OF HIS CHARACTER

*verse 140: Your word is very **pure**;*
Therefore Your servant loves it.

When something is said to be pure then it means that there is absolutely no mixture nor any flaw in it. God hates mixtures. God's Word is very pure, it is absolutely perfect, without anything useless or any fallibility! It teaches and demands purity to be manifested in our daily lives. Because the Word is pure, it is also a purifier; it cleanses from sin and guilt every heart with which it comes into contact and which receives it. Jesus says to His disciples, 'You are already clean because of the word which I have spoken to you' (John 15:3). The fact that it purifies endears it to every child of God. A child of God does not wish the Word of God brought down to the level of his own imperfect character, but desires rather that his character and conduct may be gradually raised to conformity with that blessed Word.

HIS GREATNESS AND MY LITTLENESS

*verse 141: I **am small** and despised,*
Yet I do not forget Your precepts.

One of the greatest lessons we ought to learn early in our spiritual lives is that we are nothing and that Christ is everything. John the Baptist was right when he said, '*He must increase, but I must decrease*' (John 3:30). In Matthew 5:3 we read, 'Blessed are the poor in spirit, for theirs is the kingdom of heaven.' This does not mean those with a low IQ, or the mentally deficient. This poverty of spirit is essentially spiritual, not physical or material. Sometimes material poverty is related to spiritual wealth (Luke 6:20). There are two kinds of poverty:

1. the destitute beggar;

2. The believer who recognises he has and is and can do nothing of himself, but needs the Lord for everything. It is in fact the absence of pride. A humble believer will show no attitude of superiority and he is without complexes. Paul gives great encouragement for believers that have this kind of attitude, 'But God has chosen the foolish things of the world to put to shame the wise, and God has chosen the weak things of the world to put to shame the things which are mighty; and the base things of the world and the things which are despised God has chosen, and the things which are not, to bring to nothing the things that are, that no flesh should glory in His presence' (1 Corinthians 1:27-29).

HIS RIGHTEOUSNESS

verse 142: **Your righteousness** *is an everlasting righteousness,*
And Your law is truth.

'The original is better expressed thus, "Thy righteousness is righteousness everlastingly, and thy law is truth." So the Septuagint. The English translation expresses the perpetuity of the righteousness, the original expresses also the character of it. ... God's righteousness is essentially and eternally righteousness. The expressions are absolute; there is only this righteousness, and only this truth' [14].

'How delightful to join Jehovah Himself in the ascription of praise—*"Thy throne, O God, is for ever and ever; a sceptre of righteousness is the sceptre of Thy kingdom!"* (Psalm 45:6; Hebrews 1:8). ... "Every ordinance of man" (1 Peter 2:13) is connected only with time. The Divine government has a constant reference to eternity, past and to come. *"And I heard ... the angel of the waters say; Thou*

147

art righteous, which art, and wast, and shalt be; because thou hast judged thus" (Revelation 16:5). Every instance, therefore, of His righteous administration, is that display of the Divine character which constrains the adoration of heaven. ... There may be fragments of truth elsewhere found—the scattered remnants of the fall. There may be systems imbued with large portions of *truth* deduced from this *law* [as with English justice]. But here alone is it found perfect. ... How carefully, therefore, should we test, by this standard, every doctrine (1 Thessalonians 5:21)' [3].

COMFORT AND VICTORY

verse 143: **Trouble** *and anguish have overtaken me,*
          Yet Your commandments are my delights.

When we are in distress and anguish we need to realise that He is near! The whole theme of this section is His nearness. The sufferer is not defeated, nor in despair! He is delighting in the precious word of God for his comfort, and this will surely lead him on to victory! He may be buffeted, but it will only stimulate him to fight harder and better in the strength of the Lord. So the enemy defeats his own purpose. The more he inflicts distress the more the believer is driven closer to the Lord. This is indeed an enigma for the adversary of our souls. The apostle Paul was such an indomitable soul with his positive outlook on things in the most adverse circumstances, and must have often driven the devil to despair. Listen to Paul's testimony, 'But I want you to know, brethren, that the things which happened to me have actually turned out for the furtherance of the gospel' (Philippians 1:12)! Let us not give one inch of advantage to the adversary. This is indeed real victory.

KNOWING HIM

verse 144: **The righteousness** *of Your testimonies is everlasting;
Give me understanding, and I shall live.*

For the fourth and last time in this section of eight verses
we read of righteousness. We have seen that the Lord is
righteous, that all His acts are acts of righteousness, and
that His word is righteous. Our pupil in the School of the
Spirit of God is learning fast! No doubt it is because he is
conscious of his ignorance and he repeatedly asks that he
may be given understanding. See verses 34 and 73. The
cry for understanding and knowledge is not a cry of the
'little child' in 1 John 2, whose spiritual perception is just
blossoming, but the cry of the 'fathers ... (who) have
known Him who is from the beginning' (1 John 2:13-14).
There is no end to this knowing, for our Lord is infinite!
The Lord Jesus Christ said to His Father in John 17:3,
'And this is eternal life, that they may know You, the only
true God, and Jesus Christ whom You have sent.' In
knowing Him there is Life with a capital L. 'Give me
understanding, and I shall live', says the Psalmist. My dear
friend, do you have *Life*? Eternal Life in Jesus Christ?

PSALM 119

Division Seven

ק

19. QOPH – verses 145-152

Meaning: Axe-head

Derivation: In the Phoenician and Hebrew alpha-
                    bets the shape of this letter resembles
                    'the head of an axe' or 'the back of the
                    head'.

Numerical value: One hundred (100)

Significance: From either derivation, it may mean
                    headship.

God's Word is the basis for prayer

THE NEED FOR PRAYER

verse 145: ***I cry out*** *with my whole heart;*
              Hear me, O LORD!
              I will keep Your statutes.

We might well ask, 'Why pray, if God knows everything
about our needs anyway?' But our earthly fathers also
knew what we needed, yet we would often go to them and
ask them something. Just to be able to go to father and
talk with him reaffirms every time our father-child
relationship. It is not just the asking that is important, but
the free and happy interchange between a child and his
father that is beautiful. Our Father loves to hear our voice,
loves to see us dependent upon Him for everything. The

Psalmist is in great earnest, 'I cry out with my whole heart'! This is repeated in verse 146. Here is a man pouring out his soul before the Lord.

> *Prayer is the soul's sincere desire,*
> *Uttered or unexpressed.*

> *(James Montgomery, 1818)*

It may be as simply as a baby's cry, as eloquent as a tear, as silent as a sigh, as mighty as a tornado, as strong as love. It is like the dew of heaven resting on our spirits, a sacred sweetness distilled in our souls, the secret communion of the heart.

'Hear me, O LORD! I will keep Your statutes.' We have the wonderful assurance given to us that our prayers are heard. 'Now this is the confidence that we have in Him, that if we ask anything according to His will, He hears us' (1 John 5:14). It does not say that He necessarily answers us immediately, but for the surrendered believer it is enough that the Father has heard, He will answer at the right time!

THE SUBJECT OF PRAYER

verse 146: **I cry out to You;**
      Save me, and I will keep Your testimonies.

Here the prayer is more precise and definite – 'Save me.' If we pray to the Lord to save us, it does not mean that we need to be saved from the penalty of sin a second time. It is not this kind of salvation that we are dealing with in this verse. ' "salvation" (*soteria*) is used in the New Testament for:

a)   material and temporal deliverance from danger and apprehension;

b)   of the spiritual and eternal deliverance granted immediately by God to those who accept His conditions of repentance and faith in the Lord Jesus, in Whom alone it is to be obtained;

c) of the present experience of God's power to deliver from the bondage of sin;

d) of the future deliverance of believers at the Parousia of Christ for His saints, a salvation which is the object of their confident hope, etc.' [15].

As Spurgeon puts it so precisely, ' "Save me" from the dangers which surround me, from the enemies that pursue me, from the temptations which beset me, from the sins which accuse me' [13].

THE MOMENT OF PRAYER

verse 147: **I rise before** *the dawning of the morning,*
And cry for help; I hope in Your word.

In Psalm 130:6 we read, 'My soul waits for the Lord more than those who watch for the morning'! This is indeed the secret of spiritual revival – prayer! One is often asked, 'When is the best time for prayer and quiet time?' The Bible gives the answer, 'My voice You shall hear in the morning, O LORD; in the morning I will direct it to You, and I will look up' (Psalm 5:3). Again, in Psalm 88:13 we read, 'But to You I have cried out, O LORD, and in the morning my prayer comes before You.' But what about us? You and me? How seriously do we take this necessity of praying? We do not forget to wash our face, clean our teeth and take breakfast in the morning, yet do we leave the house without praying? Jesus Christ, the sinless Son of God, often felt it necessary to get up a great while before day, and go somewhere quiet in order to pray (Mark 1:21-35). In the Gospel of Luke it is mentioned seven times that He prayed on different occasions. Can you find those occasions?

THE LENGTH OF PRAYER

*verse 148: My eyes **are awake through** the night watches,*
That I may meditate on Your word.

The night watches were specific periods during the night. The nation of Israel knew three night watches:

1. From sunset (about 6 pm) to 10 pm (Lamentations 2:19);
2. The 'middle watch', from 10 pm to 2 am (Judges 7:19);
3. From 2 am till sunrise (1 Samuel 11:11).

Under the Romans there were four night watches, agreeing with the changing of the Roman guards, each being of three hours' duration, from sunset to sunrise. They were sometimes called 'evening', 'midnight', 'cock-crowing', and 'morning'. See Matthew 14:25; 24:43; Mark 6:48; 13:35; Luke 12:38. Did the Psalmist actually start his praying before two o'clock, early in the morning? We know that Daniel prayed three times each day. The Muslims pray five times each day and also are called to prayer just before day dawns.

We can learn something from the regularity of these night watches: we also need a regular time set aside to pray. Prayer is vital in the maintenance of continuous revival. Furthermore, a time of prayer should be followed by 'meditation on the Word'.

THE PLEA OF PRAYER

*verse 149: Hear **my voice** according to Your lovingkindness;*
O LORD, revive me according to Your justice.

The Psalmist was much less privileged than we are. He didn't have that wonderful promise given to us in 1 John 5:14, 'Now this is the confidence that we have in Him, that if we ask anything according to His will, He hears us.'

To plead on the basis of God's loving-kindness, is equivalent to asking 'in the name of the Lord Jesus', God's gracious gift. Notice what the Psalmist asks for, 'Revive me.' It is precisely because Jesus Christ was given as the Saviour of the world, that all who in true repentance and faith come to Him may receive not just life, but abundant life (see John 10:10). We need this daily reviving and strengthening with might by His Holy Spirit in our inner man, so that we might experience spiritual revival. We need this reviving in order to stand fast against the wiles of the enemy.

THE REASON FOR PRAYER

verse 150: **They draw near** *who follow after wickedness;*
They are far from Your law.

William Cowper wrote, in a poem entitled 'Exhortation to Prayer', that:

> *Restraining pray'r, we cease to fight;*
> *Pray'r makes the Christian's armour bright;*
> *And Satan trembles, when he sees*
> *The weakest saint upon his knees.*

The enemy will do everything he can in order to hinder the believer from praying. So he 'draws near, who follows after wickedness'! But we can resist him, steadfast in the faith, and he will flee from us! It is prayer that moves the hand that moves the world. James says, 'You ask and do not receive, because you ask amiss' (James 4:3). But Jesus says, 'Ask, and it will be given to you; seek, and you will find; knock, and it will be opened to you. For everyone who asks receives, and he who seeks finds, and to him who knocks it will be opened' (Matthew 7:7-8). But we must learn to ask in accordance with His will, and that can only be possible when our own will has been yielded to Him. Those who follow after wickedness are characterised by lawlessness, 'they are far from Your law', they are insubordinate, and enemies to God's purposes (Romans 8:7). So as long as we remain dependent upon Him, and maintain sweet communion with Him in prayer, we have nothing to fear from the enemy.

THE COMFORT OF PRAYER

*verse 151: You **are near**, O LORD,*
And all Your commandments are truth.

If in the previous verse the enemies were near to do us mischief, what a comfort we have in this verse when we read that the Lord is near to those who put their trust in Him. Let us always remember what the apostle John says in 1 John 4:4, '*He* who is in you is greater than he who is in the world.' We are more than conquerors through our Lord Jesus Christ. Hallelujah! Sometimes our faith is weak and we see the circumstances rather than the Lord, just like Elisha's young man who saw an overwhelming enemy. Then Elisha said, '"Do not fear, for those who are with us are more than those who are with them." ... Then the LORD opened the eyes of the young man, and he saw' (2 Kings 6:16-17). It is the word of God that tells us of His nearness, but if we do not read it regularly we shall miss this sense of His presence. The Psalmist saw this also and said, 'all Your commandments are truth.'

THE FOUNDATION FOR PRAYER

verse 152: Concerning Your testimonies,
*I have known **of old** that You have founded*
them forever.

The Psalmist is sure of God's testimonies. We saw in our Introduction that 'testimony' is one facet of the Word which shows us what God is, and what we ought to be. Knowledge of what God has said and still says through His word is, of course, of the utmost importance. But knowledge puffs up. Paul knows that and warns about it. But Paul would insist that simply knowing is not enough; he wants both Timothy and ourselves to be convinced of what we have learned. See 2 Timothy 3:14, 'But you must continue in the things which you have learned and been assured of.' We must have convictions about the truth of the Word, and we must be sure about the One Who gave the Word, and also that He answers prayer that is founded on the Word and the promises He has given.

ר

20. RESH – verses 153-160

Meaning: Head or Beginning

Derivation: The word *resh* means 'head' and refers
                    to the form of this letter in the
                    Phoenician alphabet. It follows in fact
                    the outline of the back of the head.

Numerical value: Two hundred (200)

Significance: It has the significance of headship or
                    leadership. The word Russia comes
                    from its root, and may mean that Russia
                    is at the head of the Godless nations
                    (Ezekiel 38:2).

                    Resh then denotes 'to be at the head', 'at
                    first'. It is interesting to note that the
                    first word of the Bible in Hebrew is
                    b'rēsh-ith ('In the beginning'), which is
                    derived from *rōsh* (head), the '*b*'
                    meaning 'in'. It is thus a wonderful
                    reference to the true Headship of Jesus
                    Christ. Satan opposes this with all his
                    might. In the end-time he will therefore
                    use Russia to oppose Christ collectively
                    with other enemy nations.

God's Word teaches us Jesus Christ is Lord

HE KNOWS

verse 153: **Consider** *my affliction and deliver me,*
For I do not forget Your law.

The Psalmist pleads for two things:

a. consideration of his misery; and
b. deliverance from it.

He bases his plea upon the fact that he has not forgotten God's Law. The desire for sympathy is very real here. Let us remember that there was One Who also cried for sympathy and pity in His affliction, 'I looked for someone to take pity, but there was none; and for comforters, but I found none' (Psalm 69:20). He was abandoned for our sakes and for our sins, as He was made the victim – the sin-offering – having been made sin for us, that we should become the righteousness of God in Him. Now, as great High Priest, He intercedes for us in Heaven, and fully sympathises with our infirmities and weakness, but never with our sin(s). He really does consider our afflictions! He knows perfectly well all that happens to us. It is His loving hand that allows things to happen to us. Of Israel it was said 'I have surely seen the oppression of My people who are in Egypt, and ... I know their sorrows' (Exodus 3:7). He is the same today! He does sympathise and He does deliver too! It is for us to be occupied with His precious Word and not to forget it.

HE INTERCEDES

verse 154: **Plead** *my cause and redeem me;*
Revive me according to Your word.

'In all their affliction He was afflicted, and the Angel of His Presence saved them; in His love and in His pity He redeemed them; and He bore them and carried them all the days of old' (Isaiah 63:9). How this verse expresses His tender care and interest in each of His redeemed ones! He is not indifferent to the sufferings and afflictions of His own! He identifies Himself with us in our needs. It is right for us to pray for reviving, especially as our strength is but small and in affliction we get worn out. 'That He would grant you, according to the riches of His glory, to be strengthened with might through His Spirit in the inner man' (Ephesians 3:16). The Psalmist is very conscious of his weakness. Three times he cries for 'reviving' (verses 154, 156, 159), whilst he pleads his dependence upon the word of God 'according to Your word'. 'We have an Advocate with the Father, Jesus Christ the righteous' (1 John 2:1). We know we have an 'accuser', but 'he who has been born of God keeps himself, and the wicked one does not touch him' (1 John 5:18).

HE SAVES

*verse 155: Salvation **is far** from the wicked,*
For they do not seek Your statutes.

What a dreadful contrast we have in this verse! In the preceding verse we see the Psalmist pleading for the deliverance which was sure to come, but here there is no hope given of deliverance, but rather that 'salvation is far from the wicked'. But who are the 'wicked'? Psalm 9:17 gives us the answer, 'The wicked shall be turned into hell, and all the nations that forget God.' So by the 'wicked' are meant all those who leave God out of their lives and reckoning. 'If anyone does not have the Spirit of Christ, he is not His' (Romans 8:9). Yet we read in Psalm 145:18-19, 'The Lord is near to all who call upon Him, to all who call upon Him in truth. He will fulfil the desire of those who fear Him; He also will hear their cry and save them.' Let us remember, dear reader, a precious verse in Hebrews

7:25, 'Therefore He is also able to save to the uttermost those who come to God through Him, since He always lives to make intercession for them.'

HE IS MERCIFUL

*verse 156: Great are **Your tender mercies**, O LORD;*
Revive me according to Your judgments.

Here is first of all the tenderness of God's greatness, but also the greatness of God's tenderness! His mercies are great and abundant in many respects: they endure for ever and they reach unto the heavens. His mercies are also tender. '... His compassions fail not. They are new every morning: great is Your faithfulness' (Lamentations 3:22-23). Our Father is infinitely patient and long-suffering, slow to get angry, quick to forgive and ready to show mercy. 'The Lord is merciful and gracious, slow to anger, and abounding in mercy' (Psalm 103:8). Psalm 130:4 says, 'But there is forgiveness with You, that You may be feared.' It is true that the Lord is always ready to forgive when we have grieved Him in any way, and we confess our sin. The fact that He forgives should not make us careless, but rather create in us a holy fear of grieving Him. We also should ask the Lord daily to revive us about our estimation of sin, so that we might hate it. In addition, we need to be revived in our spirits to love the Lord with a greater and deeper devotion.

HE PROTECTS

*verse 157: **Many** are my persecutors and my enemies,*
Yet I do not turn from Your testimonies.

The word of God tells us that we must expect to be persecuted for Christ's sake. 'Yes, and all who desire to live godly in Christ Jesus will suffer persecution' (2 Timothy 3:12). Here again we find a contrast – the many mercies of verse 156, over against the many enemies of this verse.

'Many are the afflictions of the righteous, but the LORD delivers him out of them all. He guards all his bones; not one of them is broken' (Psalm 34:19-20). Strange that a godly man like king David, and also our Lord Jesus Christ Himself, should have so many enemies! The disciple cannot be loved, where his Master is hated! 'If the world hates you, you know that it hated Me before it hated you. ... They hated Me without a cause', are the very words of our Lord Jesus to all His disciples (John 15:18, 25). How precious it is therefore to have the assurance, '... He who is in you is greater than he who is in the world' (1 John 4:4). At such times when we are under stress and persecuted it is best to be occupied with the Word of God, 'yet I do not turn from Your testimonies.' How blessed we are when we can say with the apostle Paul, '... no one stood with me, but all forsook me. ... But the Lord stood with me and strengthened me' (2 Timothy 4:16-17).

HE KNOWS THE REBELLIOUS

verse 158: ***I see*** *the treacherous, and am disgusted,*
Because they do not keep Your word.

The Psalmist is very zealous for the honour of God. He was far more grieved by the fact that so many dishonour the Lord and have a contempt for the word of God, than by the fact that they persecuted him. God's glory was dearer to him than life itself. Let us remember that we were once transgressors and rebels, and that the Lord loved us in spite of this and saved us. Did not He 'endure such hostility from sinners against Himself' (Hebrews 12:3)? Did not He, when nailed to the cross by transgressors, pray for them, 'Father, forgive them, for they do not know what they do' (Luke 23:34)? He was grieved at their sinfulness. How often we see in the Gospels the Lord Jesus 'grieved' at the hardness of men's hearts (Mark 3:5). He had compassion on the transgressors; do we feel that same compassion for lost souls around us? The Psalmist said in verse 136, 'Rivers of water run down from my eyes, because men do not keep Your law.' Have we ever wept for the soul of a lost sinner?

HE REVIVES

verse 159: **Consider** *how I love Your precepts;*
Revive me, O LORD, according to Your loving-kindness.

The Psalmist has repeatedly cried to the Lord to be revived – see verses 25, 37, 40, 88, 107, 149, 154, 156 and 159. It is a felt need for revival! How we need to pray for this ourselves daily, 'Revive me, O LORD.' Jesus said in John 10:10, 'I have come that they may have life, and that they may have it more abundantly.' It is this more abundant life that we need. No doubt this will be our experience as we read and study the Word of God and are taught by the Holy Spirit to put it into practice. How often we become apathetic in our spiritual lives, and lack spiritual energy and vigour. Our souls cling so easily to the dust of this world (see verse 25). We need the Spirit to revive us. Notice the Psalmist did not say, 'how I perform Your precepts', but how he loved them. We often fail in many ways, but we still love the Word.

HE IS FAITHFUL

verse 160: **The entirety** *of Your word is truth,*
And every one of Your righteous judgments
endures forever.

If the word of God is truth from the beginning, then it must be eternal truth in its character and results: like its author in every particular, enduring for ever. We read in verses 89-90, 'Forever, O LORD, Your word is settled in heaven. Your faithfulness endures to all generations.' This is the rock on which our lives are built. Here is the rock of my confidence. How could we rest our hope on any salvation that did not proceed from the unchangeable mind and Word of God? What assurance could we have elsewhere? No, our trust is in the ever faithful One. The Word of God we believe to be entirely inspired, God-breathed. Every word, every jot and tittle (2 Timothy 3:16).

21. SHIN – verses 161-168

Meaning: Tooth

Derivation: This letter looks like a row of teeth. The word *shen* means a tooth, ivory or a sharp projection.

Numerical value: Three hundred (300)

Significance: A tooth cuts and tears, it pierces and crushes and pulverises. These different actions may indicate either a positive or a negative process. In this section we get the idea of persecutions (verse 161), but also of victory and peace. There is to be found 'great spoil' in this precious Word of God (verse 162, N.Tr.).

God's Word for power and peace in persecution

WE HAVE PERSECUTION

verse 161: **Princes** *persecute me without a cause,*
           But my heart stands in awe of Your word.

We know that Satan is called, 'the prince of the power of the air, the spirit who now works in the sons of disobedience' (Ephesians 2:2). He is the instigator behind all other princes who have persecuted the righteous. Think of such princes as Pilate, Felix, Festus, Nero, Hitler, etc. These men have all abused the authority invested in them by God. To be the object of persecution 'without a cause' is to be like the Master. Jesus Christ was persecuted and hated 'without a cause'. The question we must each ask ourselves, of course, is: Do I in any way provoke others to persecute me? A Christian can be obnoxious and so incite persecution against himself. But it is Peter in his First Letter who helps us accept persecution as we should (1 Peter 2:19-20; 3:17; 4:12-16). Those in high places who abuse their authority would impose their demands unjustly. We have the example of the apostles in the Book of the Acts 5:29, and the right way to react to these princes, 'We ought to obey *God* rather than men.' They stood in *awe* of God, not wanting to grieve *Him*, rather than standing in awe of the perverters of justice. Let us be animated by the same spirit, 'but my heart stands in awe of Your word.'

WE HAVE THE SWORD OF THE SPIRIT

*verse 162: I **rejoice** at Your word*
As one who finds great treasure.

We ought not to be ignorant of Satan's devices. 'For we do not wrestle against flesh and blood, but against principalities, against powers, against the rulers of the darkness of this age, against spiritual hosts of wickedness in the heavenly places' (Ephesians 6:12). Against such princes we must take up 'the sword of the Spirit, which is the Word of God' (Ephesians 6:17). How would we be motivated to take up that sword if we have found no joy in it? The Psalmist rejoiced at that word, as 'one who finds great treasure'. We have to get to know that word so that the Holy Spirit can bring it to our remembrance when faced with conflict. When Satan sends his fiery darts against us, we must be able to handle the shield of faith to quench these darts, and by using the Word of God against him: that is what the Bible says. Bible-study is therefore of the utmost importance for every believer. The Hebrew word translated here as 'treasure' literally means 'plunder' or 'spoil'. The degree of my joy in God's word is expressed here as being spoil, the fruit of conflict. We have used the word of God in conflict and carried away the victory and great spoil; our spiritual lives have been enriched.

WE MUST STAND FIRM AND RESIST

*verse 163: I hate and abhor **lying**,*
But I love Your law.

This is the attitude of the 'new man' in the language of the New Testament. 'These six things the Lord hates, yes, seven are an abomination to Him: ... a false witness who speaks lies ...' (Proverbs 6:16, 19). By nature we hate what God loves, and we love what God hates (see Romans 7:18 etc.)! Are we as Christians sometimes living a lie? Think of David in 1 Samuel 21:2, 13; 27:10! He lived a lie every day for a long period! How miserable he must have been! God was not with him in those days to bless him, even though God protected him in His mercy. Notice the opposites in this verse, 'hate' ... 'love'. The more I love His Word, the more I shall hate sin in any form. Let us remember that exaggeration is a form of lying; do we sometimes gloss over things, tell a white lie or half truths, or make false excuses? Let us therefore double our energy in studying the word of God, that 'the word of Christ dwell in us richly' (Colossians 3:16), and so be fitted for spiritual warfare, able to resist the enemy, so that he will flee from us. We dare not compromise, or live double lives but we must live transparent lives in the centre of God's will.

WE HAVE PERFECT JOY

verse 164: **Seven** *times a day I praise You,*
Because of Your righteous judgments.

How often we have been encouraged by that wonderful verse 28 in the Letter to the Romans, chapter eight, 'And we know that all things work together for good to those who love God, to those who are the called according to His purpose.' This verse is a commentary on the expression here called 'righteous judgments'. Does not the assurance that God does all things well and justly, give us cause for praising Him? Yes, we have every reason for always praising Him. 'Be thankful', says Paul in Colossians 3:15. He means that we should always have this attitude of being thankful for everything. In verse 17 Paul exhorts us to utter our thankfulness audibly, 'giving thanks to God the Father through Him.' The expression seven times would perhaps indicate the frequency of the habit. It is like living a life of perpetual praise. Do we give thanks before every meal we take, even if we are having it in a public place somewhere, like a restaurant? What an opportunity for rendering a silent testimony. This giving of thanks, and praise, is not optional, not as and when we feel like it. It is an obligation, it is God's will, 'In everything give thanks; for this is the will of God in Christ Jesus for you' (1 Thessalonians 5:18).

WE HAVE PERFECT PEACE

verse 165: Great **peace** *have those who love Your law,*
And nothing causes them to stumble.

'You will keep him in perfect peace, whose mind is stayed on You, because he trusts in You' (Isaiah 26:3). Even in the midst of conflict and persecutions the believer can enjoy this inner peace. 'Be anxious for nothing, but in everything by prayer and supplication, with thanksgiving,

169

let your requests be made known to God; and the peace of God, which surpasses all understanding, will guard your hearts and minds through Christ Jesus' (Philippians 4:6-7). Let us remark first of all that the Psalmist does not say, 'great peace have those who perfectly keep Your law', but 'who love Your law'. This is the desire of the new nature in us. When we really want to do the will of God we have deep serenity and peace. The verse continues, 'and nothing causes them to stumble.' Nothing can injure them (Romans 8:28). I must let nothing hinder this peace from ruling in my heart. I submit totally to His will and have peace and true happiness. We must neither give offence nor take offence. 'Blessed are the peacemakers' (Matthew 5:9)!

WE HAVE PERFECT CONFIDENCE

*verse 166: LORD, **I hope** for Your salvation,
And I do Your commandments.*

For the believer hope is not something uncertain or doubtful, but sure and certain. 'For we were saved in this *hope*, but hope that is seen is not hope; for why does one still hope for what he sees? But if we hope for what we do not see, we eagerly wait for it with perseverance' (Romans 8:24-25). 'Now may the God of hope fill you with all joy and peace in believing, that you may abound in hope by the power of the Holy Spirit' (Romans 15:13). The salvation we know in the New Testament is both temporal (that is, salvation from circumstances) and an eternal salvation of the soul. We also wait for the final salvation of our bodies, and this is the 'blessed hope' of the Christian. When we live daily in the expectation of that blessed hope to be fulfilled in the coming of the Lord Jesus to take us home to the Father's House, we shall want to be found doing His commandments. 'By this we know that we love the children of God, when we love God and keep His commandments. For this is the love of God, that we keep His commandments. And His commandments are not burdensome' (1 John 5:2-3). We must therefore hope in God, and do what is right. These two must never be separated. 'The first without the second would be mere presumption: the second without the first mere formalism' [13].

WE MUST BE PERFECTLY OBEDIENT

*verse 167: My soul **keeps** Your testimonies,*
And I love them exceedingly.

You cannot keep or remember what you do not have or have not learned. The Psalmist knew the Word and meditated upon it often, no doubt. Do we? How much do we love His word? It has been said, 'We must love it better than the wealth and pleasure of this world' [7]. The 'soul' is expressive of the whole personality. He says his whole being kept God's word: spirit and soul and body were under the control of the word! Verses 167 and 168 combined say that the Psalmist kept the testimonies as well as the precepts carefully. Remember in the Introduction I said that the 'testimony' is that which testifies of what God is, and of what we ought to be; whereas the 'precept' is a charge given to us by God for which we are responsible.

> *Trust and obey, for there's no other way*
> *To be happy in Jesus, than to trust and obey.*

Notice the intensity of his devotion to the word, '… I love … exceedingly'! As C H Spurgeon remarks, 'He did not merely store up revealed truth by way of duty, but because of a deep unutterable affection for it. He felt that he could sooner die than give up any part of the revelation of God. The more we store our minds with heavenly truth, the more deeply shall we be in love with it: the more we see the exceeding riches of the Bible, the more will our love exceed measure, and exceed expression' [13].

GOD HAS A PERFECT PATH FOR US

*verse 168: **I keep** Your precepts and Your testimonies,*
For all my ways are before You.

'All my ways are before You', says the Psalmist! All our pathway and our footsteps are known by our Father and He ponders them. What a thought!

Division Eight

ת

22. TAU – verses 169-176

Meaning: Sign or Cross

Derivation: It was a sign in the form of a cross branded on the thigh or neck of horses and camels, whence the name of the letter *tau*, which in Phoenician, and on the coins of the Maccabees, has the form of a cross.

Numerical value: Four hundred (400)

Significance: This is the last letter of the alphabet. It means a 'sign', a sign in the form of a cross (Ezekiel 9:4, where it is called a 'mark' – 'put a mark'). If the first letter of the Hebrew alphabet, *aleph*, signifies an ox, which animal was offered as a burnt-offering, and points symbolically to the Person of the Son of God, signifying the greatest form of appreciation of the Person of the Lord Jesus, then Psalm 119 comes to a conclusion in this last letter *tau*, symbol of that shameful cross on which He who was the sacrifice for sin was nailed.

Appendix: God's Word for continuous revival

This eighth section divides into four plus four. The first four verses speak of perseverance and the last four of prayer or a plea for salvation. In the first place this 'Appendix' speaks prophetically of Israel in the tribulation of the last days. This will be the time of their spiritual re-birth as a nation for Jehovah, when they come into the New Covenant (the 8th). Christians already taste its blessings now!

PERSEVERANCE IN PRAYER

*verse 169: Let my cry **come** before You, O LORD;*
Give me understanding according to Your word.

This section also prefigures the repentance of the true Remnant of Israel in a future day. 'The people [of Israel] … acknowledge that they had gone astray [verse 176], (for that is their case and is the condition of the whole Psalm, the law being now written, in desire at least, in their hearts), and gone astray like a sheep wholly lost. The humbled and repentant remnant (and, I repeat, we, when we have wandered from God), look for God's seeking them, for they were upright in heart, mindful of His commandments. This gives the key to the whole Psalm —Israel gone astray, the desire and love of God's law in their hearts, but *their* circumstances and condition not yet set right by Jehovah's deliverance, but their hearts set right that He may come in His word, and His deliverance being their desire, and His word the ground of their hope. … We are far away from Christian ground here. Nothing makes it more sensible than the Psalms. Neither the Father, nor divine righteousness, is known in them, nor that whole class of feelings, blessed and holy as those feelings are, which flow from them. May we remember we are

Christians!' [4]. Literally, 'Let my cry come near before You', is the earnest cry of the heart here. Many had been his cries and supplications (verses 145-152), but now his petition is that they might come near before Him, and that nothing would block the way. We must let nothing hinder our prayers. Married couples are reminded that they are 'heirs together of the grace of life, that your prayers may not be hindered' (1 Peter 3:7). He prays that God would give him understanding, so that he might know how to behave himself whilst in trouble. Our every petition should be urged upon the assurance of His promise.

PERSEVERANCE IN SUPPLICATION

*verse 170: Let my supplication **come** before You;*
Deliver me according to Your word.

We should therefore pray according to His will, and according to what He has promised in His word. He will answer such supplications. Supplication is asking for myself, whilst intercession is asking on behalf of others. The Psalmist is conscious of his own dire need for deliverance. We need constant deliverance every day from sin, self and Satan. God does provide deliverance; see for instance the precious promise in 1 Corinthians 10:13, 'No temptation has overtaken you except such as is common to man; but God is faithful, who will not allow you to be tempted beyond what you are able, but with the temptation will also make the way of escape, that you may be able to bear it.'

PERSEVERANCE IN PRAISE

*verse 171: My lips **shall utter** praise,*
For You teach me Your statutes.

This man pleads first (verse 170) (see Luke 18:1-8); then sings (verse 171), preaches (verse 172), travails (verse

173), and longs (verse 174). He has consecrated lips (verse 171), a consecrated tongue (verse 172), soul (verse 175), and feet (verse 176). In fact his whole spirit and soul and body are for the Lord, and all to be used to praise the Lord. It is very important what we actually use our lips for. Proverbs 10:19 says, 'In the multitude of words sin is not lacking, but he who restrains his lips is wise.' Notice why his lips shall utter praise, 'for You teach me Your statutes.' It is those of us who let God teach us by His Holy Spirit who have cause and material to praise Him. When God opens our understanding, He also opens the heart and the lips, so that our mouths may show forth His praise.

Perseverance in witnessing and preaching

*verse 172: My tongue **shall speak** of Your word,*
For all Your commandments are righteousness.

'Come and hear, all you who fear God, and I will declare what He has done for my soul' (Psalm 66:16). We ought to be daily witnesses to God's goodness and salvation. Do we ever witness with our lips? Remember Romans 10:9-10, 'That if you confess with your mouth the Lord Jesus and believe in your heart that God has raised Him from the dead, you will be saved. For with the heart one believes unto righteousness, and with the mouth confession is made unto salvation.' When we meet with other believers, what do we talk about? It is not enough to offer up spiritual praise to the Lord, but we should also 'preach' His word for the edification of others. Are our hearts really overflowing so that our lips speak of Him and His righteous ways? In this way what we say ministers grace to the hearers. There are many believers who never open their mouth in praise in the meeting for worship, nor in the prayer meeting. Are their hearts so empty that they have nothing to say to God? Are they so uncertain that they dare not speak of Him in public? Let all those fearful and timid ones pray this prayer, 'Lord, open Thou my lips, that my tongue may speak of Thy word' [3]. Our spiritual priesthood does not only consist in offering up 'spiritual sacrifices acceptable to God through Jesus Christ', but our royal priesthood exists to 'proclaim the praises of Him who called you out of darkness into His marvellous light' (1 Peter 2:5, 9).

HE WILL CONTINUE TO HELP

verse 173: **Let** *Your hand become my help,*
For I have chosen Your precepts.

Yes, the Lord is willing to help those who come to Him with their timidity and lack of spiritual courage to witness or to confess His name. We may all 'come boldly to the throne of grace' and 'find grace to help in time of need' (Hebrews 4:16). We need help to keep His word ('Your precepts'). When Peter wanted to walk on the waves toward the Lord Jesus and suddenly became conscious of the roaring waves, he began to sink. That very moment 'he cried out, saying, "Lord, save me!" And immediately Jesus stretched out His hand and caught him, and said to him, "O you of little faith, why did you doubt?"' (Matthew 14:30-31). 'You hold me by my right hand' (Psalm 73:23). How we depend on Him for everything! How comforting also to hear Him say to us, 'I, the LORD your God, will hold your right hand, saying to you, "Fear not, I will help you"' (Isaiah 41:13).

HE WILL CONTINUE TO SAVE

verse 174: **I long** *for Your salvation, O LORD,*
And Your law is my delight.

The Bible teaches us that there is temporal salvation from, or in, earthly circumstances, and that there is eternal salvation of the soul/spirit which we enjoy even while still on earth, and that there is the final salvation of our bodies, which is sometimes called 'the redemption of our bodies' (see Philippians 1:19; 1 Peter 1:9,5; Romans 8:23). Do we long for that final salvation, the coming of the Lord Jesus to take His Bride home? During that waiting period we shall be occupied with His precious word to obey it and walk according to its instructions. 'Your law is my delight.' This 'longing' and 'delight' mark what is characteristic of Christianity: not merely duty, but delight to do His will! As someone has said, 'Duties become privileges, when Christ is their source and life' [3].

It should be our heart's desire to be constantly close to Him. 'Whom have I in heaven but You? And there is none upon earth that I desire besides You' (Psalm 73:25).

HE WILL CONTINUE TO REVIVE

*verse 175: Let my soul **live**, and it shall praise You;*
And let Your judgments help me.

The Psalmist would like his life prolonged so that he can continue to praise God! 'For in death there is no remembrance of You; in the grave who will give You thanks?' (Psalm 6:5). It was his desire that as long as he lived he would live for the praise of God! Is that also our desire? The last six Psalms are for the most part throughout the breathings of praise. The close of Psalm 119 is also pervaded with praise. See verses 164, 171 and 172. Unless our souls are daily revived by the Holy Spirit, our lips will be silent and no praise is heard. We ought therefore to pray that He would grant us, 'according to the riches of His glory, to be strengthened with might through His Holy Spirit in the inner man' (Ephesians 3:16). We ought to be 'giving thanks always for all things to God the Father in the name of our Lord Jesus Christ' (Ephesians 5:20). The more we learn about Him and His ways, which the

Psalmist calls 'Your judgments', the more we shall be helped in our praise. A victorious Christian, enjoying abundant life in Christ, is also a singing and praising Christian! This is having the joy of our salvation (verse 174). The Psalmist did not know what we Christians have – the indwelling of the Holy Spirit. How much more reason do we have therefore to praise! We can praise God for whatever He does, and wherever He leads us!

HE WILL GUIDE TO THE END

verse 176: ***I have gone astray*** *like a lost sheep;*
Seek Your servant,
For I do not forget Your commandments.

Some commentators see in this last section (verses 169-176) Israel's regeneration in the future, their spiritual re-birth as a nation. The soul in this verse realises its lost condition; he acknowledges having gone astray (a habitual tendency), and now he looks to Jehovah as the Shepherd of Israel to seek him (although Israel has already been touched by the grace which has wrought in them to put into their hearts that desire for His commandments!). This is indeed the moral state of Israel today and in the last days – when in their land, but final deliverance has not yet come. We can also see in it a picture of any lost soul, conscious of having gone astray like a lost sheep. (It is a natural human tendency to wander and stray). Only One can save him – the Good Shepherd. But the Good Shepherd must first lay down His life for His sheep. The last letter of the alphabet, as we have seen, is the letter *tau*, which signifies a sign, or a cross. Only through Christ's death on the cross can there be any salvation for lost sheep.

Conclusion

'I do not think that there could possibly be a more appropriate conclusion of such a Psalm as this, so full of the varied experiences and the ever-changing frames and feelings even of a child of God, in the sunshine and the cloud, in the calm and in the storm, than this ever-clinging sense of his propensity to wander, and the expression of his utter inability to find his way back without the Lord's guiding hand to restore him; ... What an insight into our poor wayward hearts does this verse give us!' [2]. What a wonderful textbook we have found therefore in this precious Psalm 119.

We have found that the word of God:

1. has plentiful resources for our pilgrim path, verses 1-24,
2. and has strength for the weary, verses 25-48.
3. In it we find our immense spiritual riches, verses 49-72,
4. and through meditating upon it we grow into spiritual maturity, verses 73-96.
5. Here we are told of the importance of daily Bible study, verses 97-120,
6. for we are all students in God's school, verses 121-144.
7. Thus we can experience spiritual renewal, verses 145-168,
8. and the Holy Spirit can maintain us in a continuous spiritual revival to praise God, verses 169-176.

REFERENCES

1. John Gifford Bellett, *Short Meditations on the Psalms; chiefly in their Prophetic character*, James Nisbet and Co.: London, 1843

2. Barton Bouchier, *Manna in the Heart; or, Daily Comments on the Book of Psalms, adapted for the use of Families*, J F Shaw: London, 1855

3. Charles Bridges, *Exposition of Psalm CXIX as illustrative of the Character and Exercises of Christian Experience*, L B Seeley & Son; R B Seeley & Burnside: London, 1827

4. John Nelson Darby, *Practical Reflections on the Psalms*, R L Allan: London, 1870

5. Heinrich Friedrich Wilhelm Gesenius, *Lexicon Manuale Hebraicum et Chaldaicum in Veteris Testamenti Libros,* 1833 [*Gesenius' Hebrew-Chaldee Lexicon to the Old Testament Scriptures. Translated with additions and corrections from the author's Thesaurus and other works*, translated by Samuel Prideaux Tregelles, Samuel Bagster: London, 1846]

6. Billy Graham, *The Charlotte Observer*, September 26, 1958

7. Matthew Henry, *An exposition of the five poetical books of the Old Testament: viz. Job, Psalms, Proverbs, Ecclesiastes, and Solomon's Song,* printed by T Darrack, for T Parkhurst, J Robinson, and J Lawrence, 1710

8. George Horne, *A commentary on the Book of Psalms. In which their literal or historical sense, as they relate to King David and the people of Israel, is illustrated; and their application to Messiah, to the Church, and to Individuals as members thereof, is pointed out; with a view to render the use of the Psalms pleasing and*

profitable to all orders and degrees of Christians, ClarendonPress: Oxford, 1776

9. Thomas Manton, *God's Faithfulness from Generation to Generation in One Hundred and Ninety Sermons on the Hundred and Nineteenth Psalm,* London, 1681-1701

10. George Campbell Morgan, *Searchlights from the Word: being 1188 sermon-suggestions, one from every chapter in the Bible.* Fleming H Revell Co.: New York, 1926 [Reprinted in 1994 under the title *Life Applications from Every Chapter of the Bible*]

11. Johannes Paulus Palanterius, *Illustris Psalmorum Davidicorum Explanatio,* Brescia, 1600

12. William Graham Scroggie, *The Psalms, volume 3: Psalms 101 to 134 (Know your Bible),* Pickering & Inglis Ltd: London, 1950

13. Charles Haddon Spurgeon, *The Treasury of David containing an original exposition of the Book of Psalms; a collection of illustrative extracts from the whole range of literature; a series of homiletical hints upon almost every verse, and lists of writers upon each Psalm,* Passmore & Alabaster: London, 1870-86
The Golden Alphabet of the Praises of Holy Scripture: setting forth the believer's delight in the Word of the Lord: being a devotional commentary upon the One Hundred and Nineteenth Psalm [mainly from *The Treasury of David*], Passmore & Alabaster: London, 1887

14. John Stephen, *The Utterances of the CXIX Psalm; expounded in a series of lectures,* Robert Walker: Aberdeen, 1861

15. William Edwy Vine, *An Expository Dictionary of New Testament Words,* Oliphants: London, Edinburgh, 1940

OTHER BOOKS BY COR BRUINS

GOD AND RELATIONSHIPS

ISBN: 0-901860-36-1; Scripture Truth Publications

108 pages; Paperback; August 2006

THE DIVINE DESIGN IN THE GOSPELS

ISBN: 0-901860-31-X; Scripture Truth Publications

291 pages; Hardcover; June 1983

EVEN SO SEND I YOU

ISBN: 0-947588-08-6; Chapter Two

140 pages; Paperback; November 1985

SPEAKING BY THE SPIRIT OF GOD

ISBN: 0-901860-14-X; Scripture Truth Publications

102 pages; Paperback; September 1996

JOSHUA

ISBN: 0-901860-20-4; Scripture Truth Publications

235 pages; Paperback; June 1999

IS JESUS GOD?

ISBN: 0-901860-28-X; Scripture Truth Publications

16 pages; Paperback; July 2004

About The Author

From 1955 to 1965 Cor Bruins served the Lord in a school in Upper Egypt, before moving to Lebanon. He worked in the various churches there until 1975, when he and his family were forced to leave due to the civil war.

Cor has lived in England ever since, spending his time preparing and giving teaching ministry in Europe, the Middle East and the USA. He now describes himself as a semi-retired Christian teacher.

Cor has written several books over the past twenty-five years and has also written a variety of articles on Christian topics. He has also regularly broadcast Bible talks for the Truth For Today programme on London's Premier Radio.

He has been married to Audrey for over fifty years, and they have eight children.

Lightning Source UK Ltd.
Milton Keynes UK
UKOW04f0020251017

311561UK00001B/12/P

9 780901 860880